BRODY'S

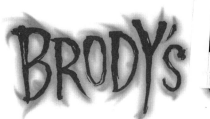

BRODY'S GHOST ™

BOOK 2

STORY AND ART BY
MARK CRILLEY

DARK HORSE BOOKS®

Publisher - Mike Richardson
Designer - Justin Couch
Assistant Editor - Patrick Thorpe
Editor - Dave Land

Published by Dark Horse Books
A division of Dark Horse Comics, Inc.
10956 SE Main Street
Milwaukie, OR 97222

darkhorse.com

To find a comic shop in your area call the Comic Shop Locator Service toll-free at (888) 266-4226

First edition: January 2011
ISBN 978-1-59582-665-7

BRODY'S GHOST BOOK 2

10 9 8 7 6 5 4 3 2
Printed at Lebonfon Printing, Inc., Val-d'Or, QC, Canada

THIS BOOK IS DEDICATED TO MY PARENTS,
WHO GAVE ME ALL THE TRAINING
I'D EVER NEED.

THE STORY SO FAR...

Brody is a young man living in a decaying metropolis a number of decades from now. After being dumped by his girlfriend, Nicole, he has allowed his life to spiral into a directionless mess, making ends meet by playing guitar on the street for loose change. His daily routine is shattered one afternoon when he finds himself face to face with a teenage female ghost, one that he alone is capable of seeing. She tells him her name is Talia, that she died five years earlier of leukemia, and that she won't be allowed into heaven until she unmasks a dangerous killer called the Penny Murderer. Talia believes Brody possesses untapped psychic powers that will allow him to hear "death echoes"—extra-sensory clues left behind at the various murder scenes. On a night when Brody has both wrecked things for good with Nicole and been badly beaten by a street gang called the L47s, Talia leads him to an old, abandoned Japanese temple on the other side of town. There she introduces Brody to an ancient samurai ghost named Kagemura, who, upon seeing dramatic proof of Brody's abilities, agrees to administer the training he will need to fully unlock his psychic powers.

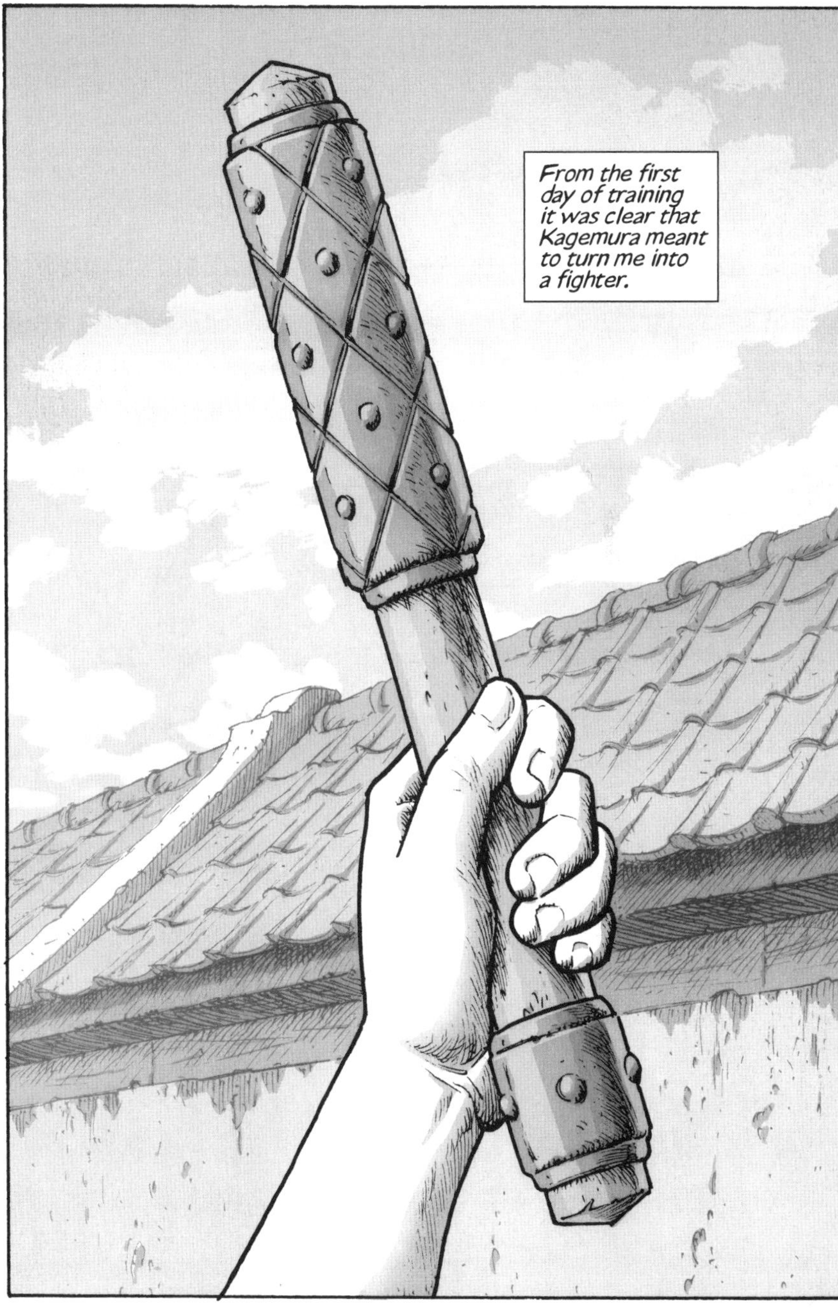
From the first day of training it was clear that Kagemura meant to turn me into a fighter.

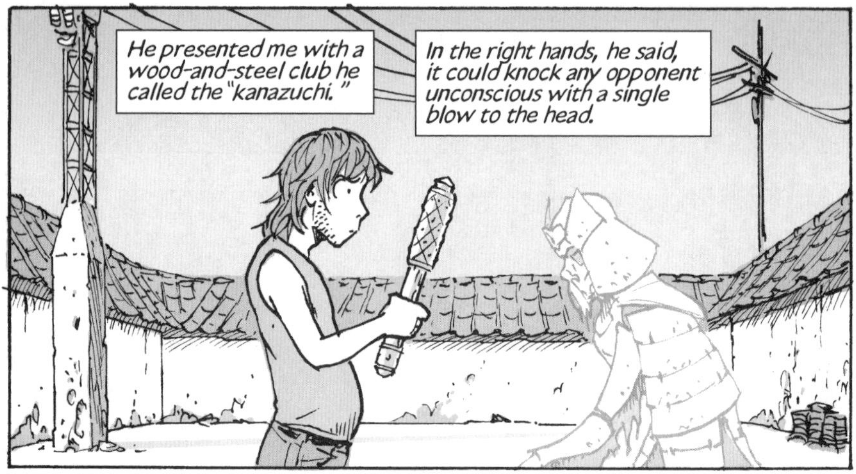

He presented me with a wood-and-steel club he called the "kanazuchi."
In the right hands, he said, it could knock any opponent unconscious with a single blow to the head.

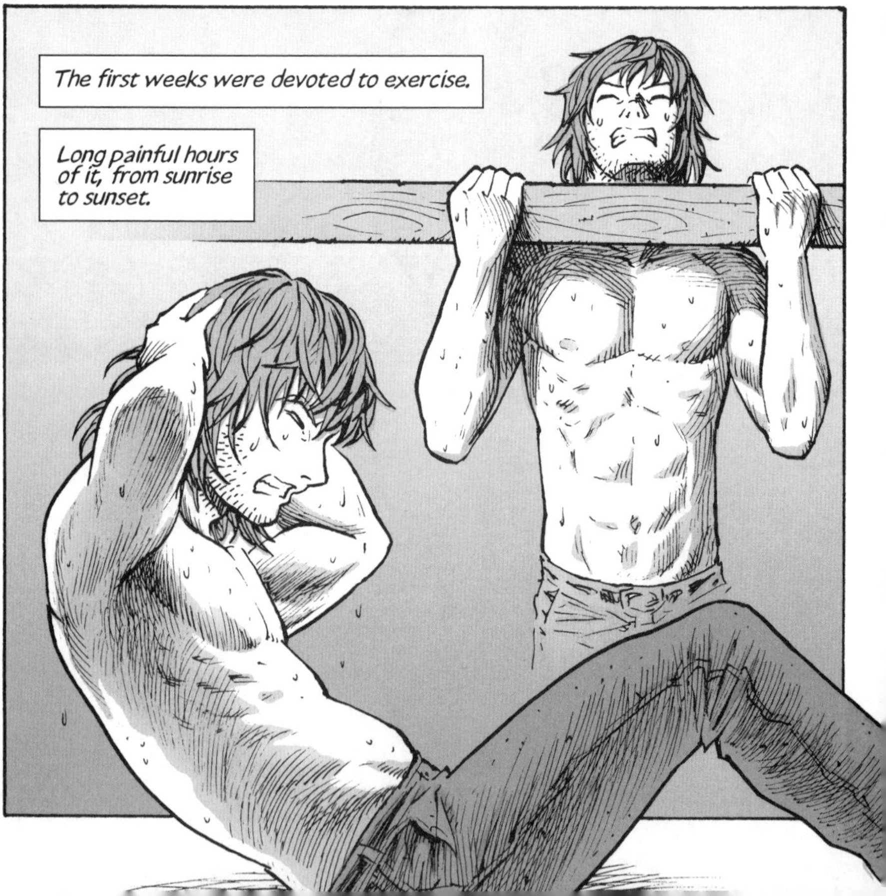

The first weeks were devoted to exercise.
Long painful hours of it, from sunrise to sunset.

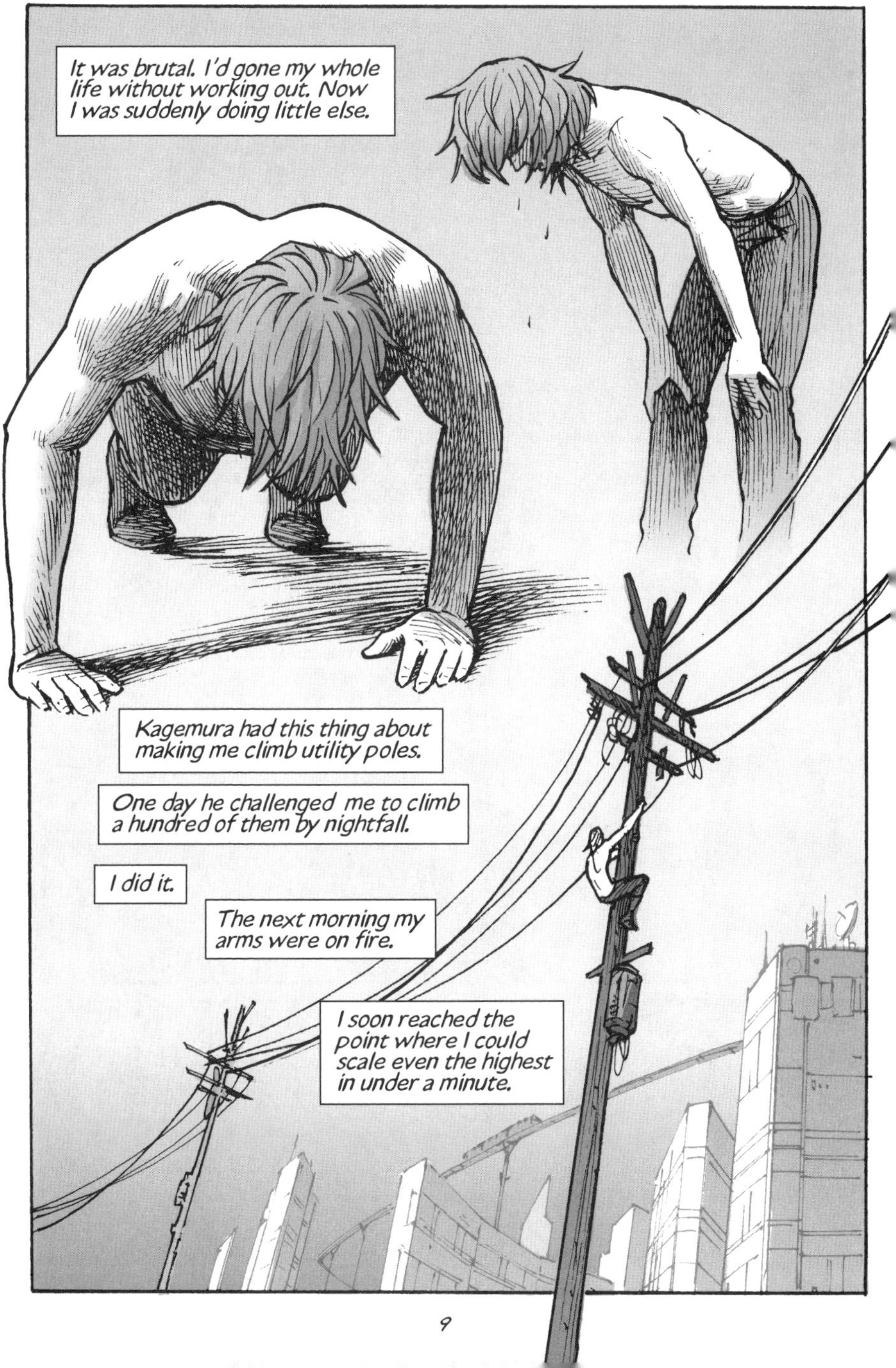
It was brutal. I'd gone my whole life without working out. Now I was suddenly doing little else.
Kagemura had this thing about making me climb utility poles.
One day he challenged me to climb a hundred of them by nightfall.
I did it.
The next morning my arms were on fire.
I soon reached the point where I could scale even the highest in under a minute.

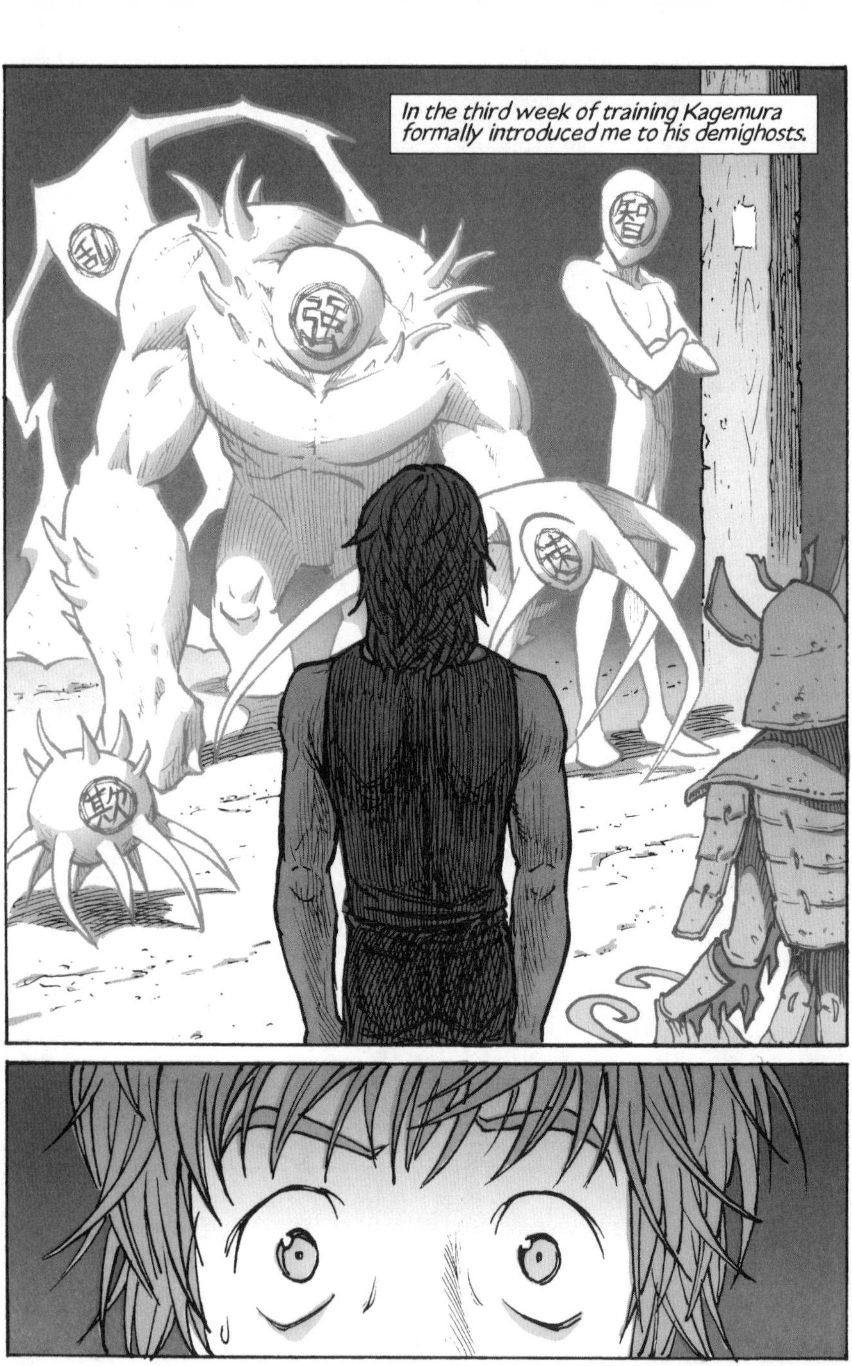
In the third week of training Kagemura formally introduced me to his demighosts.

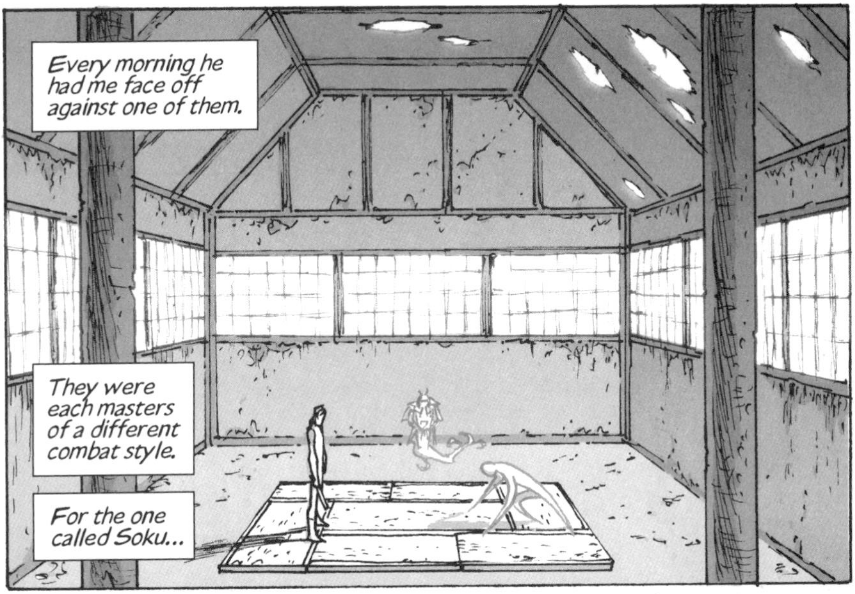
Every morning he had me face off against one of them.
They were each masters of a different combat style.
For the one called Soku...

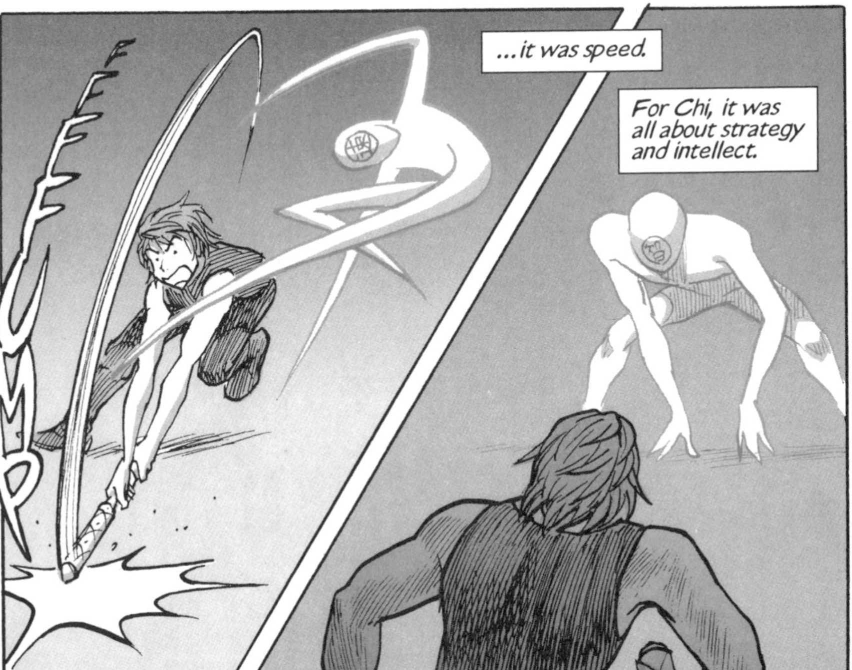
...it was speed.
For Chi, it was all about strategy and intellect.

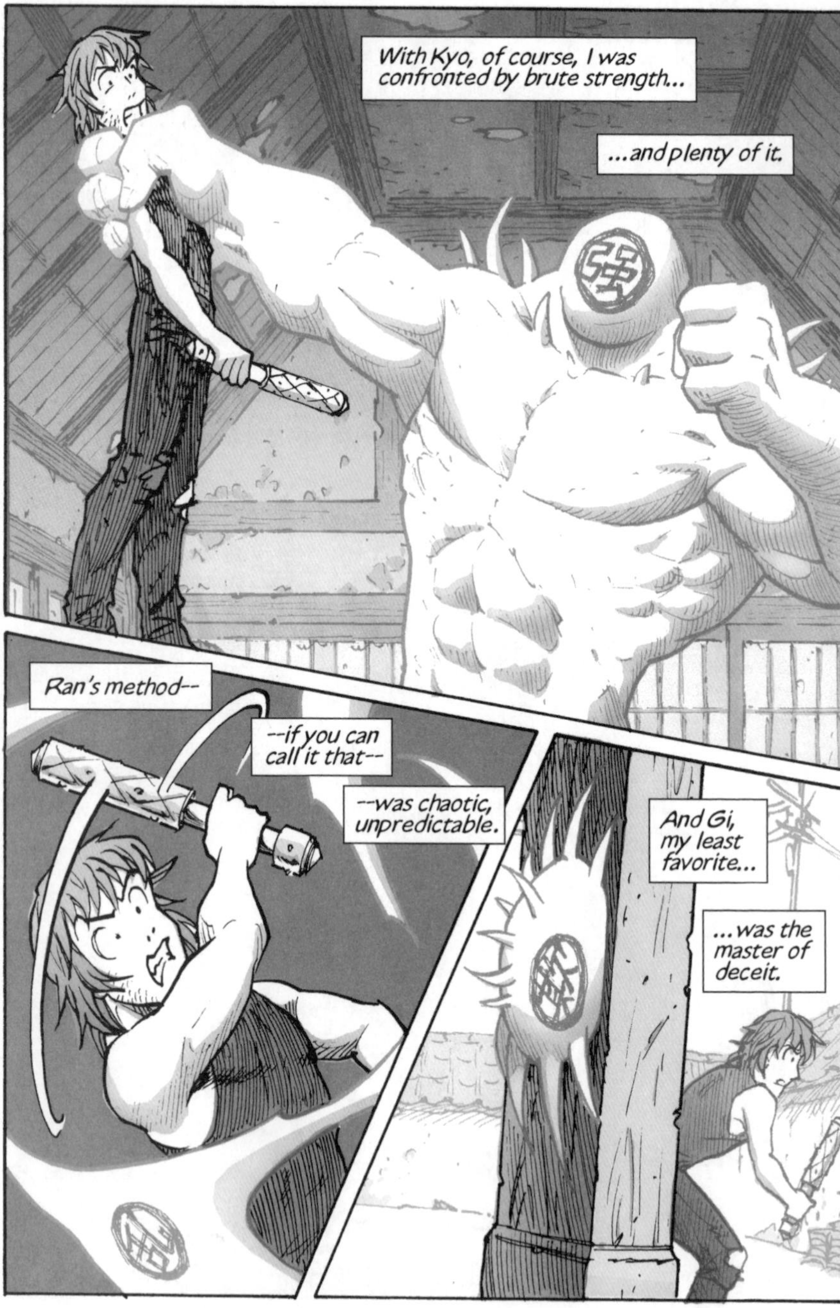
With Kyo, of course, I was confronted by brute strength...
...and plenty of it.
Ran's method--
--if you can call it that--
--was chaotic, unpredictable.
And Gi, my least favorite...
...was the master of deceit.

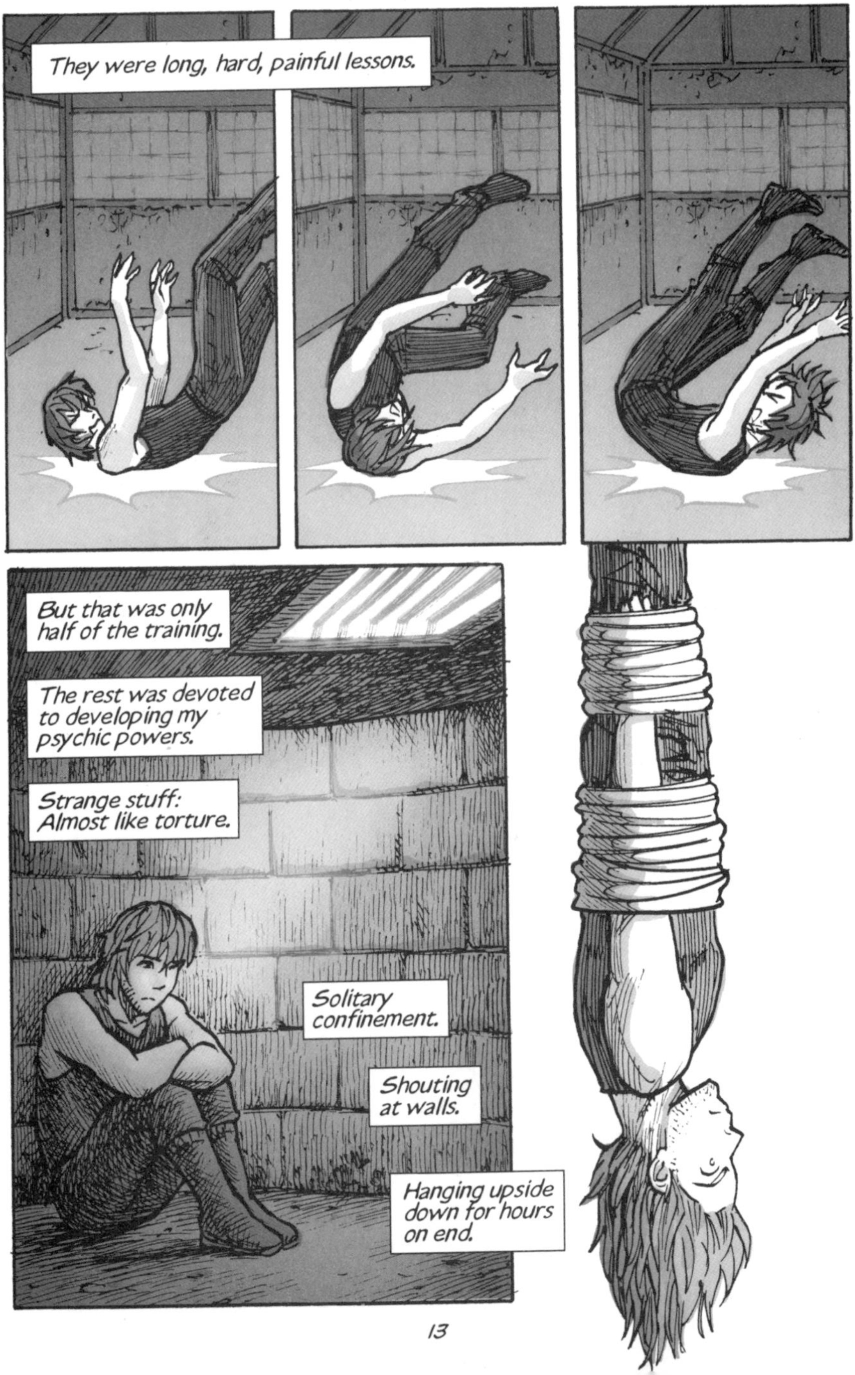
They were long, hard, painful lessons.
But that was only half of the training.
The rest was devoted to developing my psychic powers.
Strange stuff: Almost like torture.
Solitary confinement.
Shouting at walls.
Hanging upside down for hours on end.

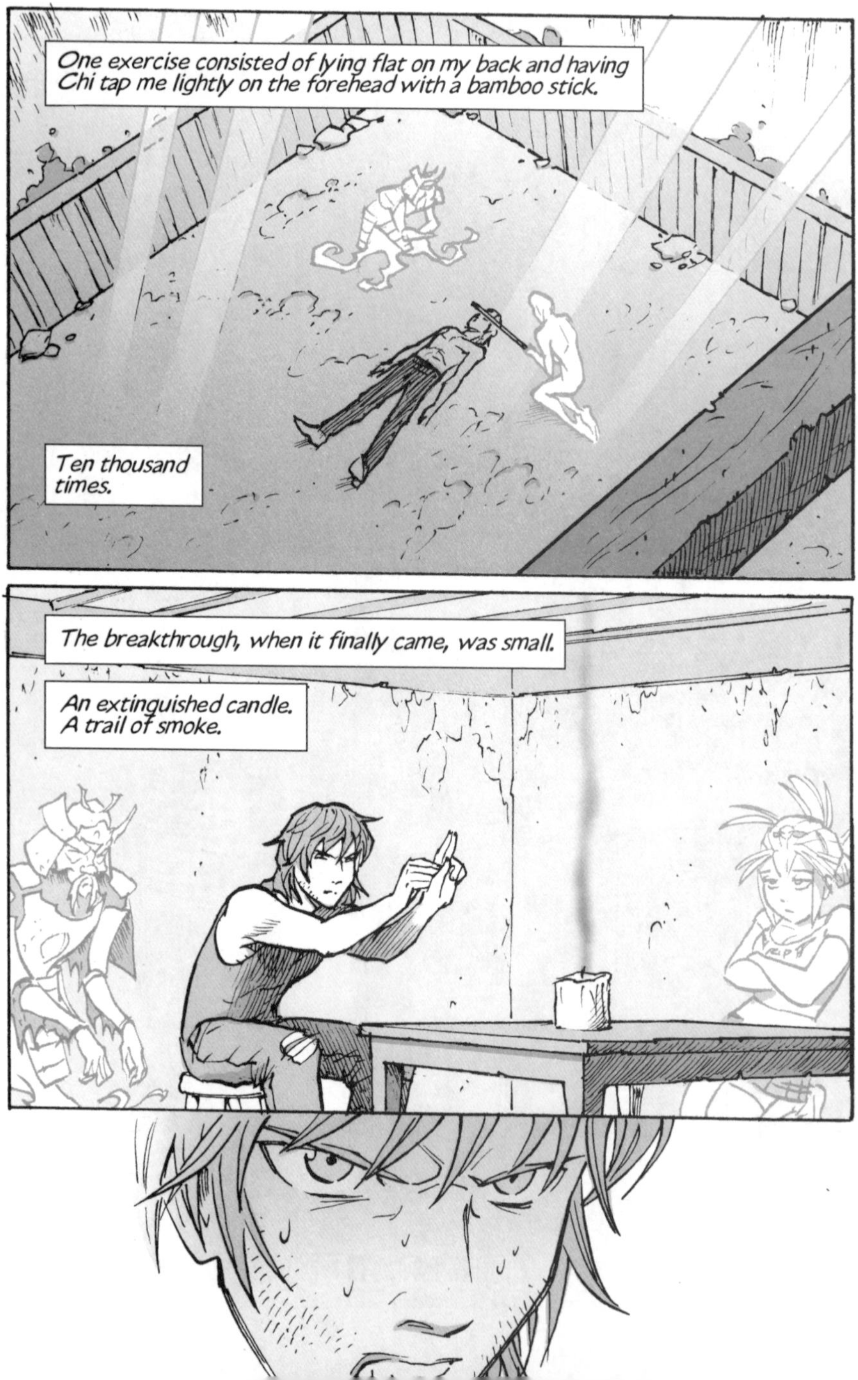
One exercise consisted of lying flat on my back and having Chi tap me lightly on the forehead with a bamboo stick.
Ten thousand times.
The breakthrough, when it finally came, was small.
An extinguished candle. A trail of smoke.

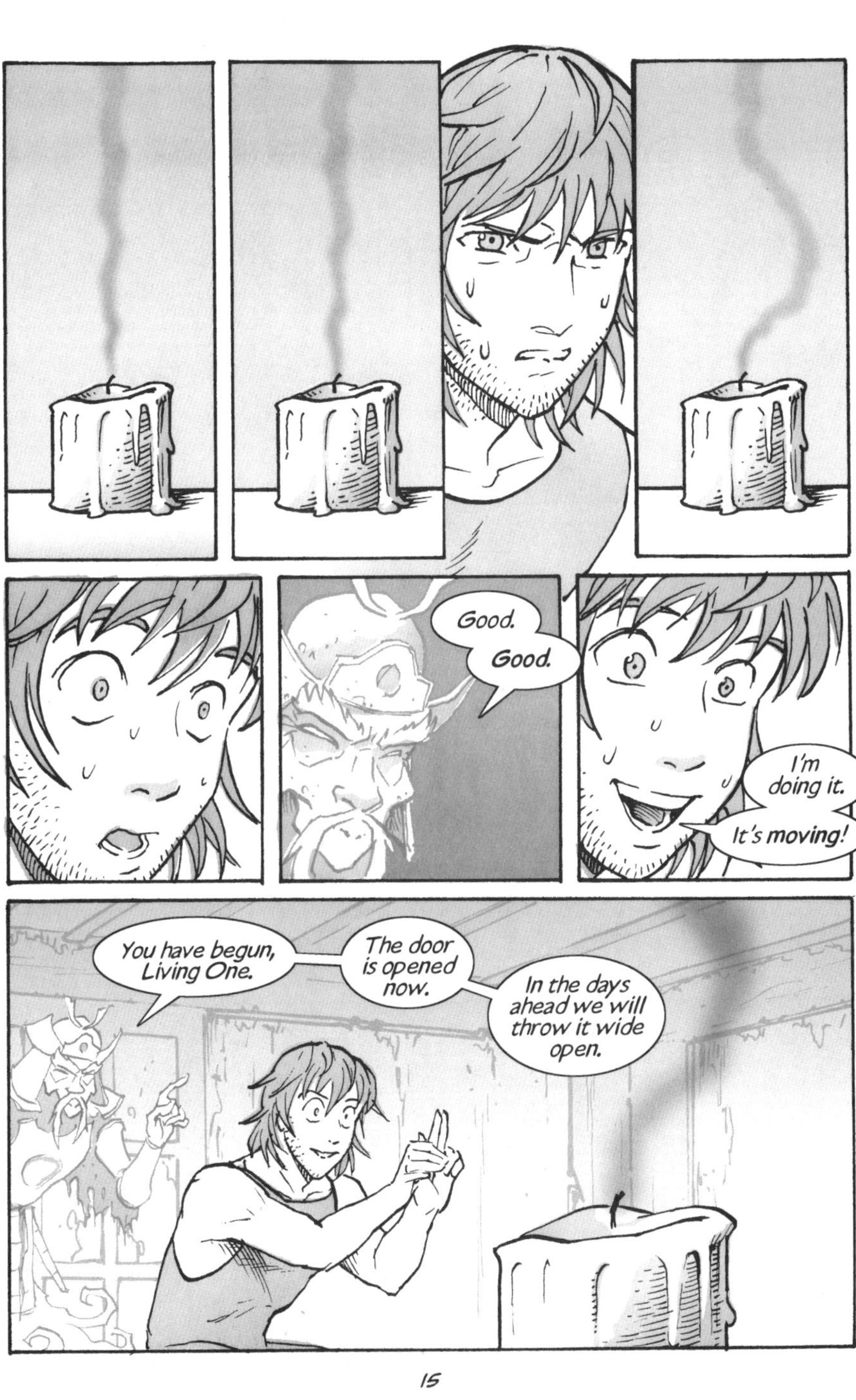
Good.
Good.
I'm doing it.
It's moving!
You have begun, Living One.
The door is opened now.
In the days ahead we will throw it wide open.

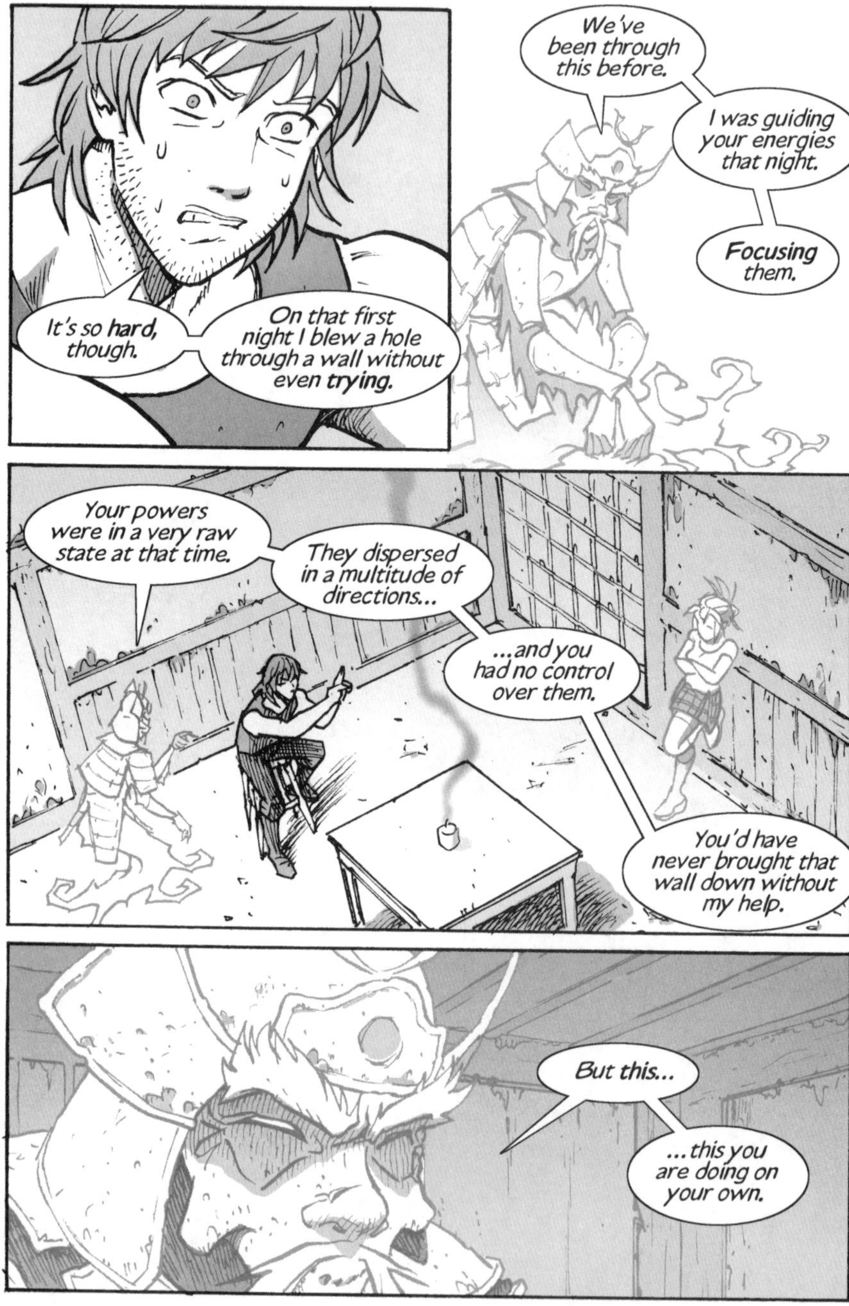
It's so hard, though.
On that first night I blew a hole through a wall without even trying.
We've been through this before.
I was guiding your energies that night.
Focusing them.
Your powers were in a very raw state at that time.
They dispersed in a multitude of directions...
...and you had no control over them.
You'd have never brought that wall down without my help.
But this...
...this you are doing on your own.

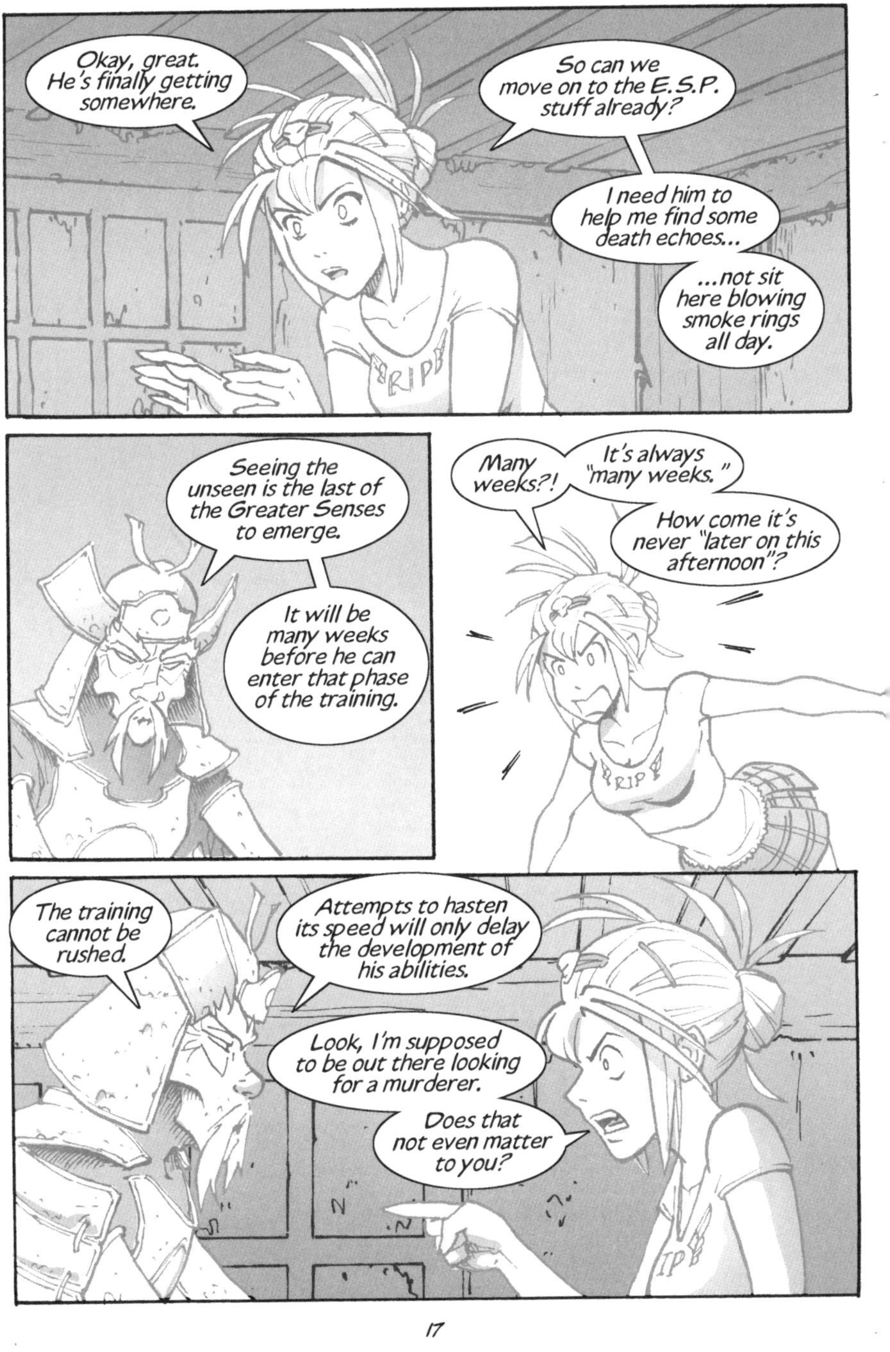
Okay, great. He's finally getting somewhere.
So can we move on to the E.S.P. stuff already?
I need him to help me find some death echoes...
...not sit here blowing smoke rings all day.
RIP
Seeing the unseen is the last of the Greater Senses to emerge.
It will be many weeks before he can enter that phase of the training.
Many weeks?!
It's always "many weeks."
How come it's never "later on this afternoon"?
RIP
The training cannot be rushed.
Attempts to hasten its speed will only delay the development of his abilities.
Look, I'm supposed to be out there looking for a murderer.
Does that not even matter to you?

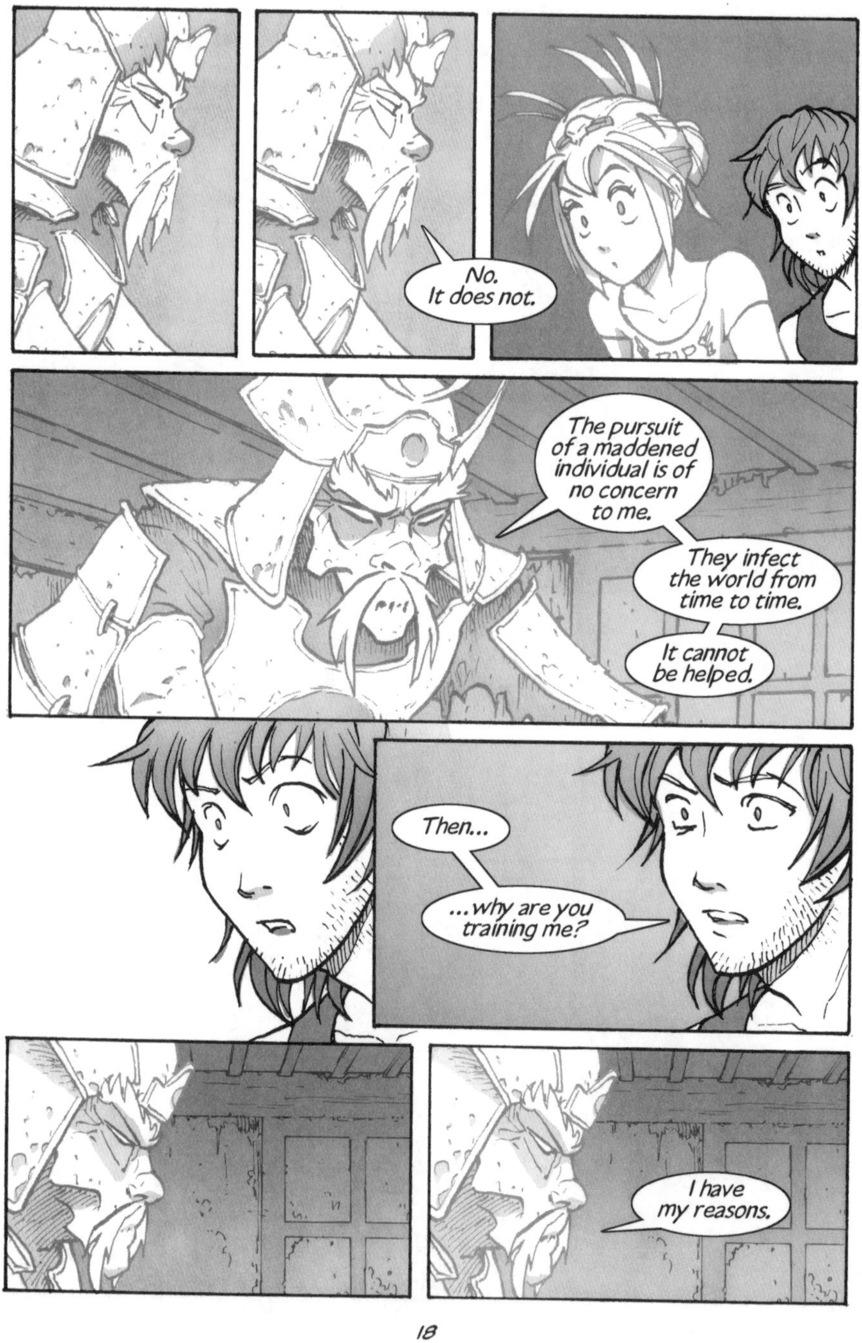
No.
It does not.
The pursuit of a maddened individual is of no concern to me.
They infect the world from time to time.
It cannot be helped.
Then...
...why are you training me?
I have my reasons.

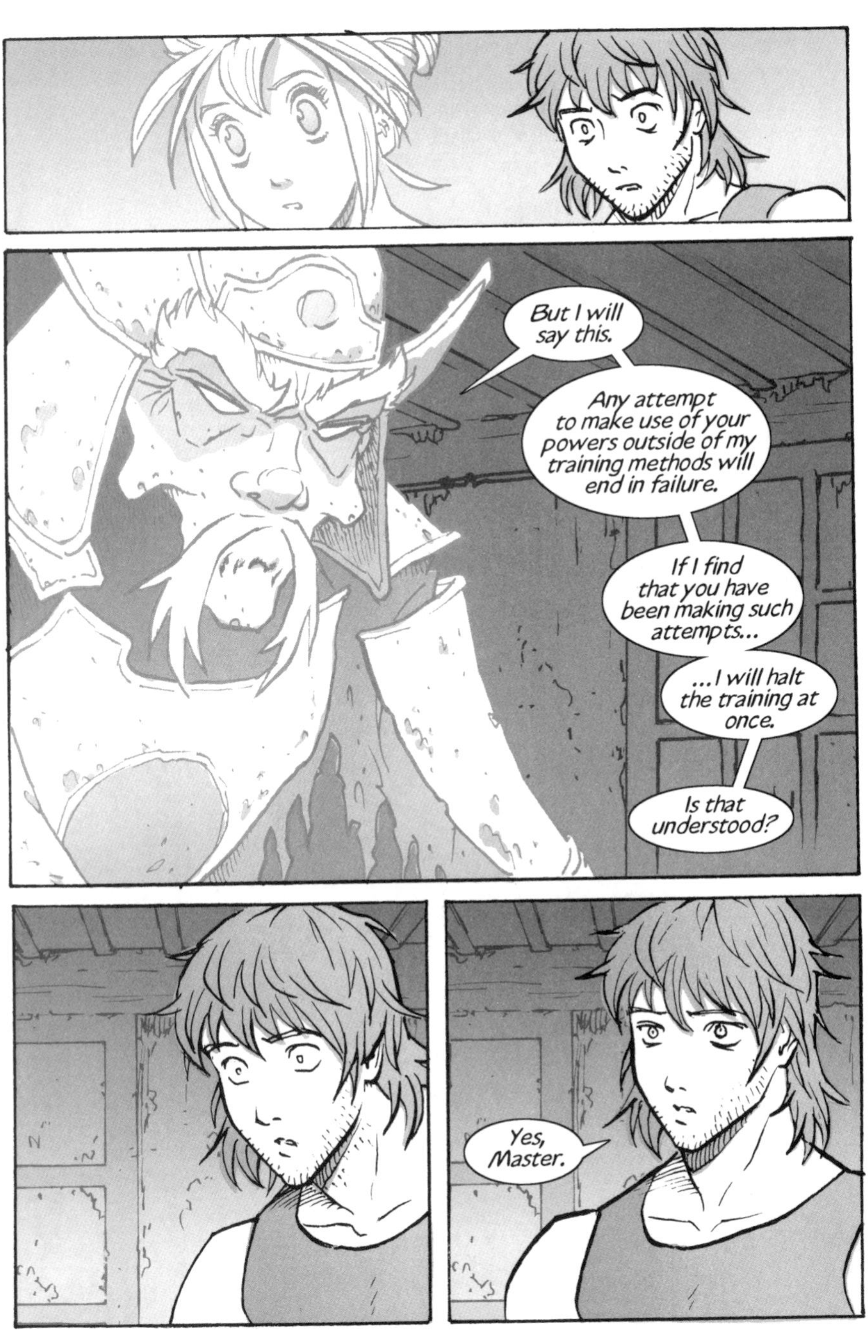
But I will say this.
Any attempt to make use of your powers outside of my training methods will end in failure.
If I find that you have been making such attempts...
...I will halt the training at once.
Is that understood?
Yes, Master.

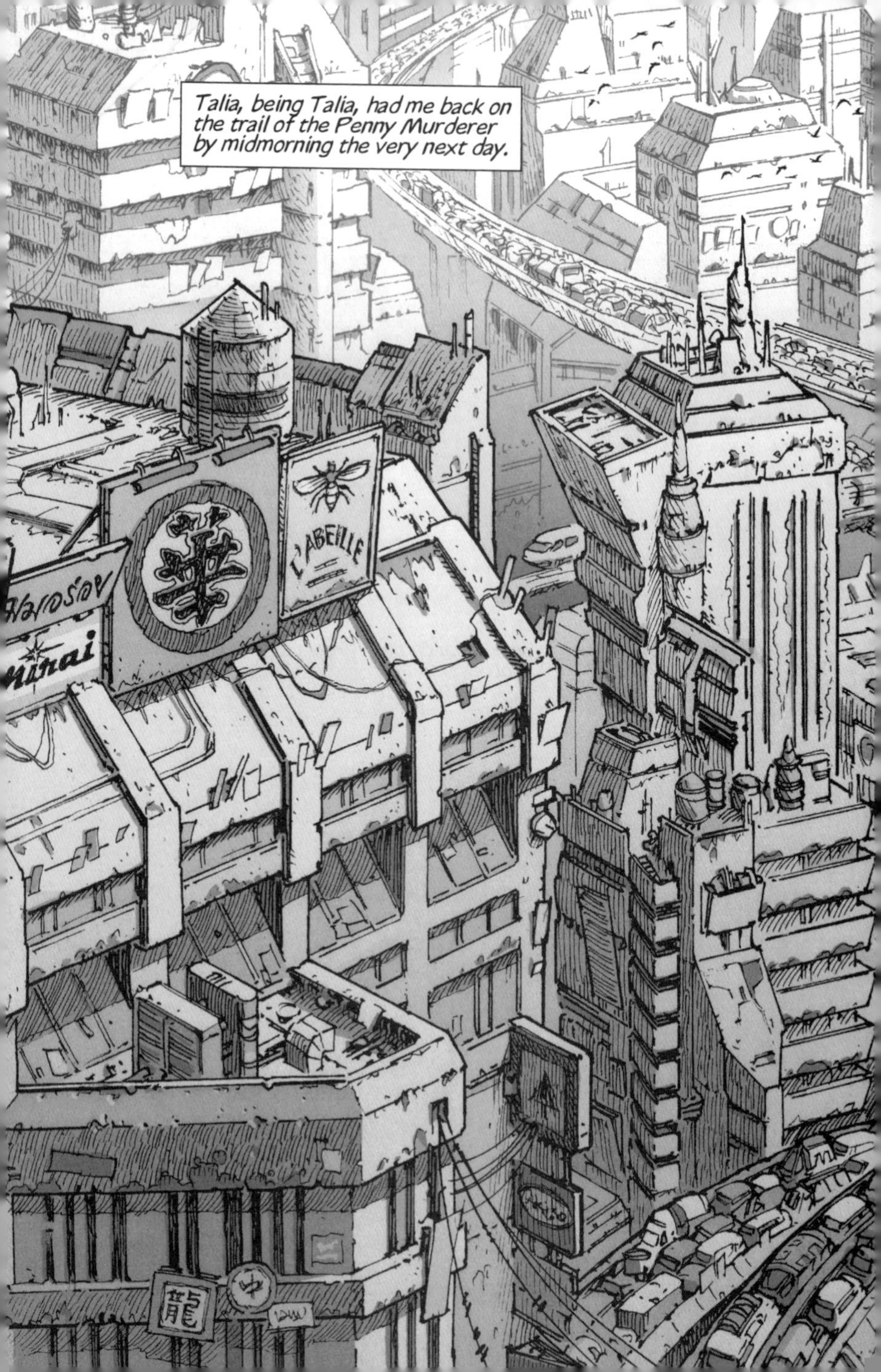
Talia, being Talia, had me back on the trail of the Penny Murderer by midmorning the very next day.
L'ABEILLE
龍

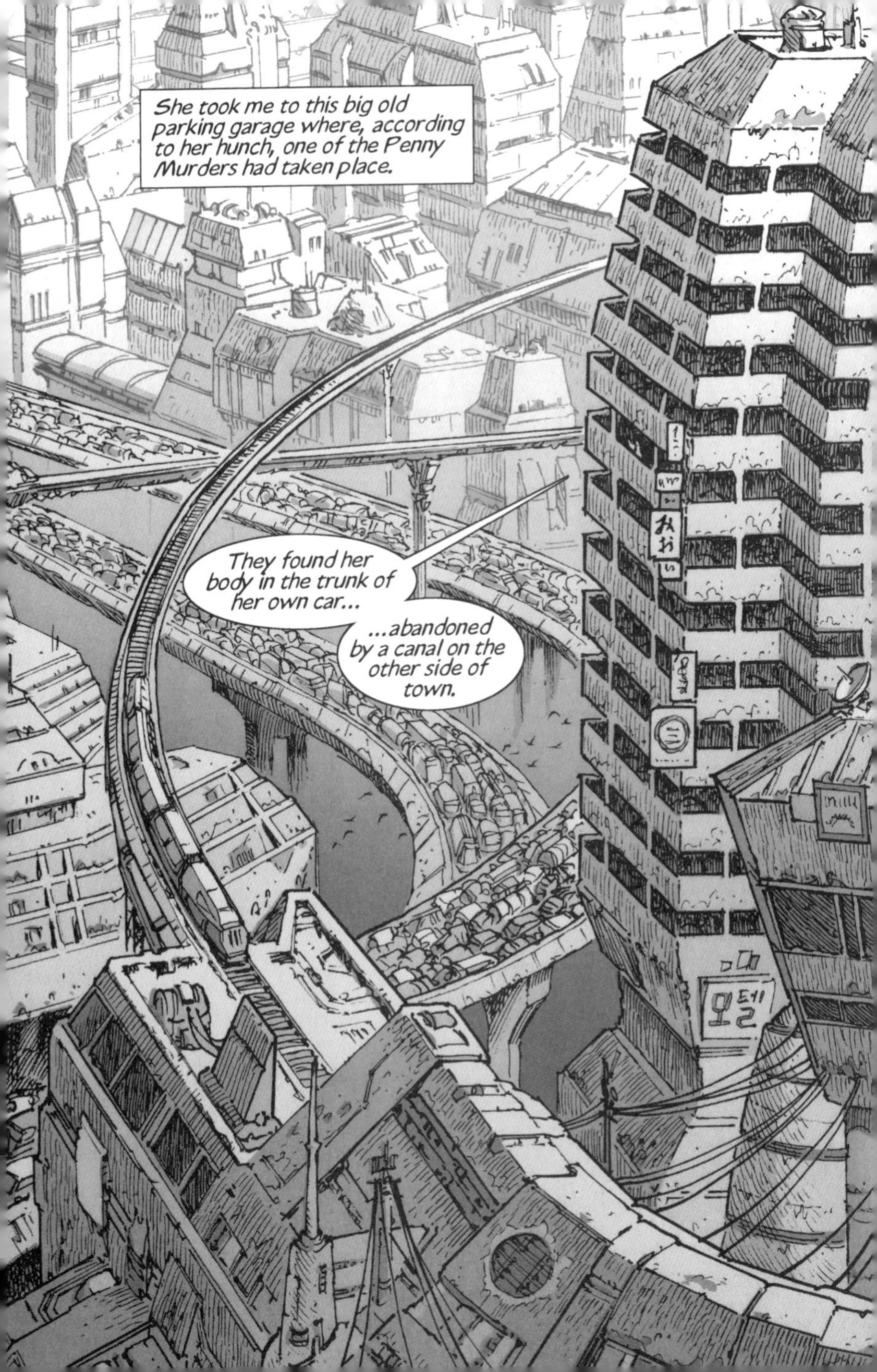
She took me to this big old parking garage where, according to her hunch, one of the Penny Murders had taken place.
They found her body in the trunk of her own car...
...abandoned by a canal on the other side of town.

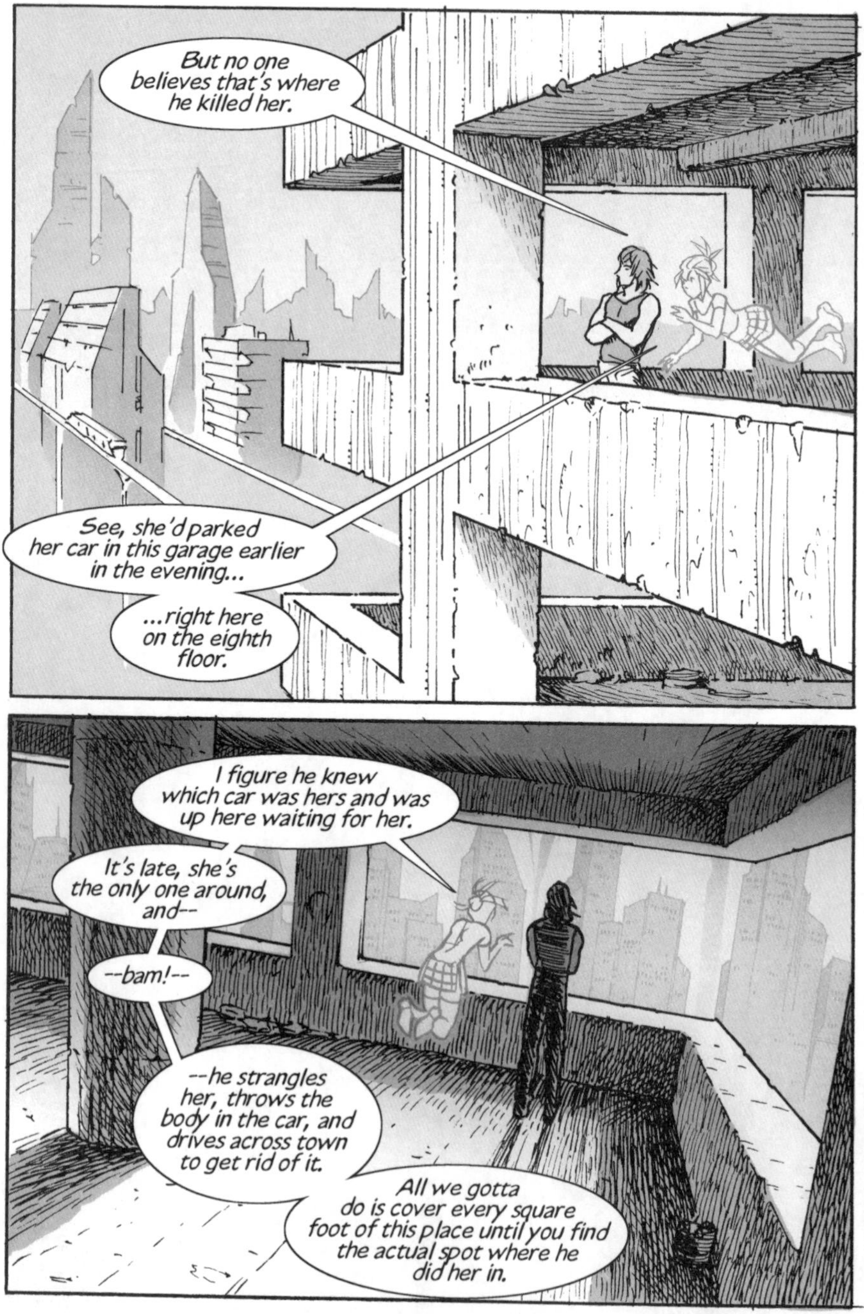
But no one believes that's where he killed her.
See, she'd parked her car in this garage earlier in the evening...
...right here on the eighth floor.
I figure he knew which car was hers and was up here waiting for her.
It's late, she's the only one around, and--
--bam!--
--he strangles her, throws the body in the car, and drives across town to get rid of it.
All we gotta do is cover every square foot of this place until you find the actual spot where he did her in.

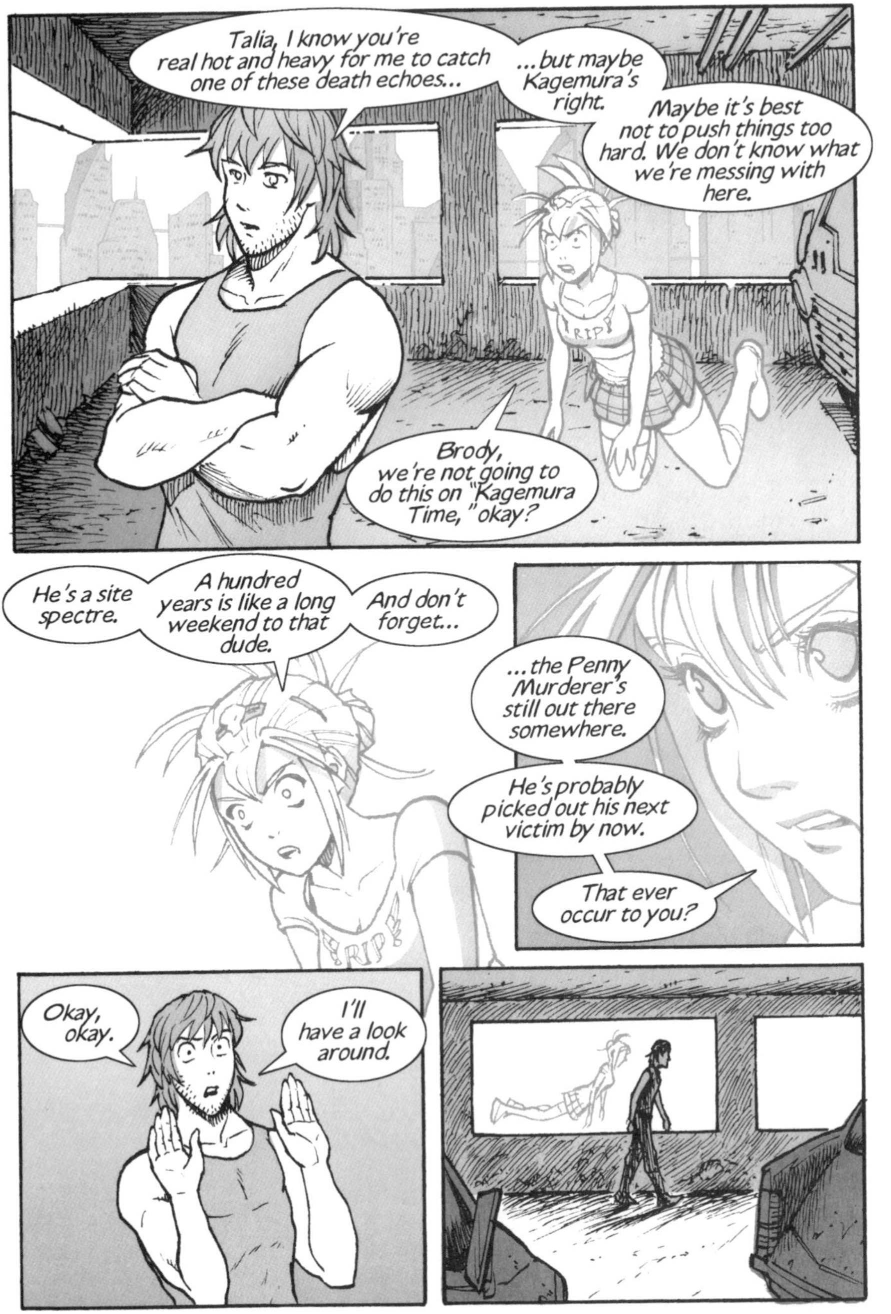
Talia, I know you're real hot and heavy for me to catch one of these death echoes...
...but maybe Kagemura's right.
Maybe it's best not to push things too hard. We don't know what we're messing with here.
Brody, we're not going to do this on "Kagemura Time," okay?
He's a site spectre.
A hundred years is like a long weekend to that dude.
And don't forget...
...the Penny Murderer's still out there somewhere.
He's probably picked out his next victim by now.
That ever occur to you?
Okay, okay.
I'll have a look around.

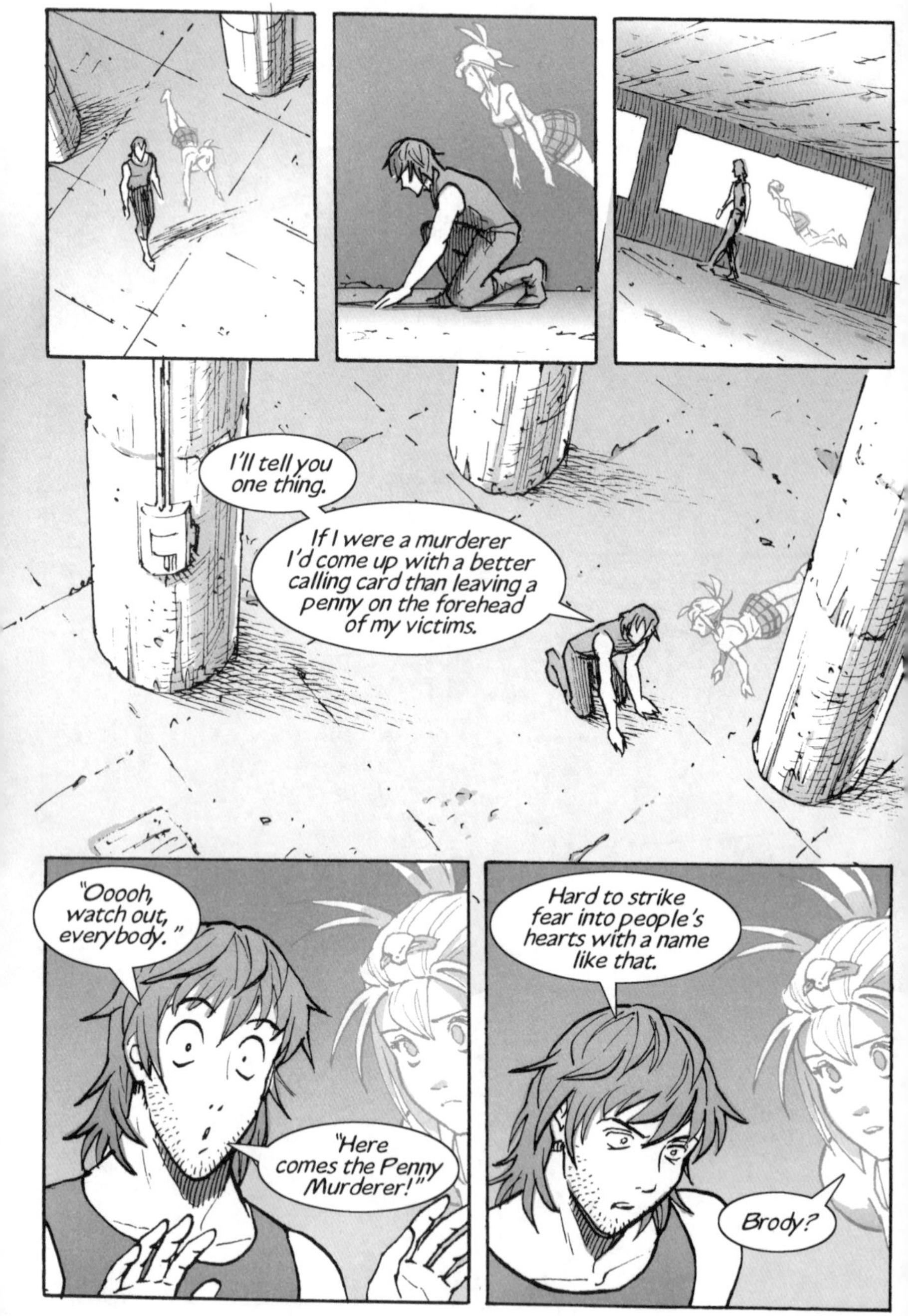
I'll tell you one thing.
If I were a murderer I'd come up with a better calling card than leaving a penny on the forehead of my victims.
"Ooooh, watch out, everybody."
"Here comes the Penny Murderer!"
Hard to strike fear into people's hearts with a name like that.
Brody?

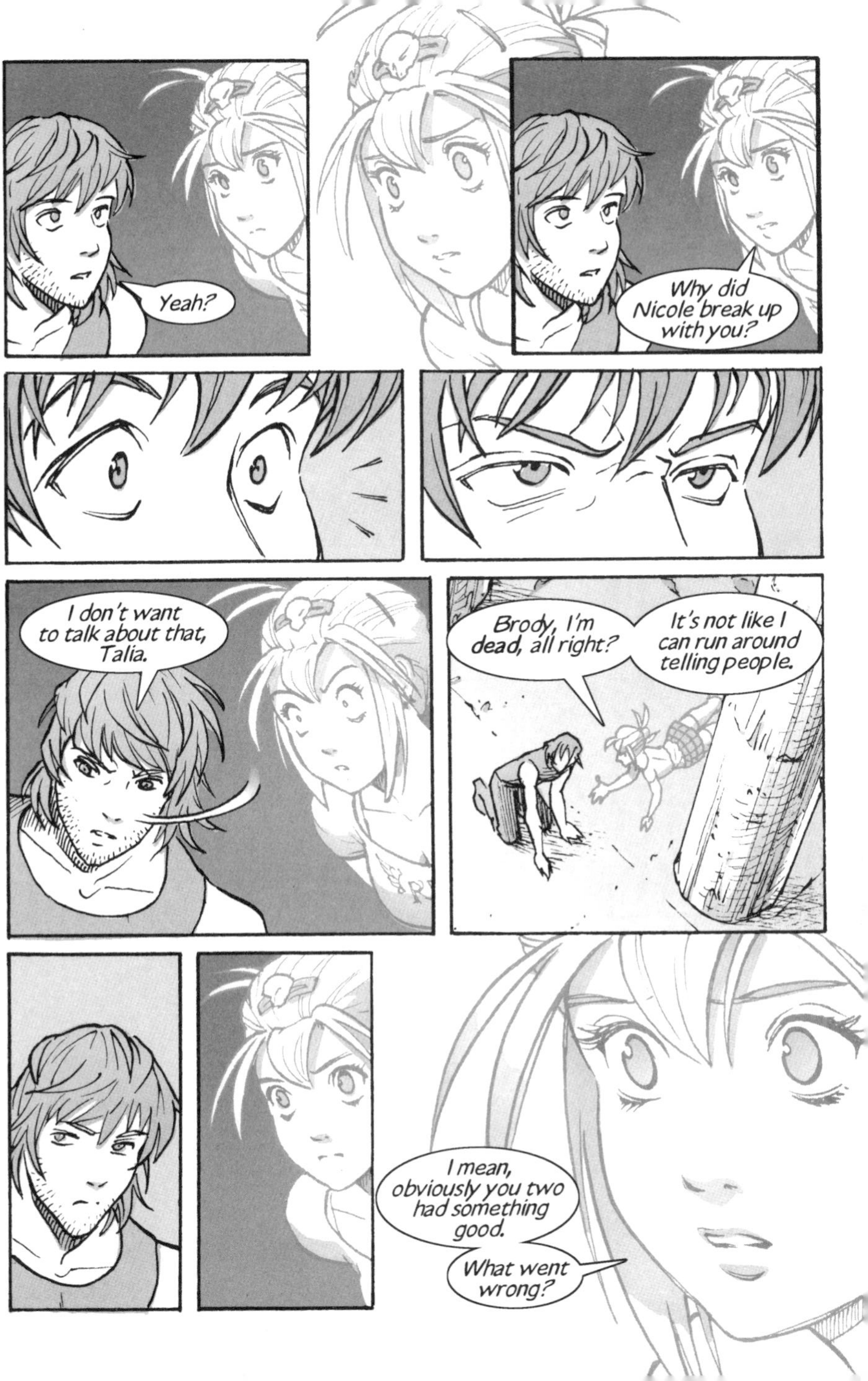
Yeah?
Why did Nicole break up with you?
I don't want to talk about that, Talia.
Brody, I'm dead, all right?
It's not like I can run around telling people.
I mean, obviously you two had something good.
What went wrong?

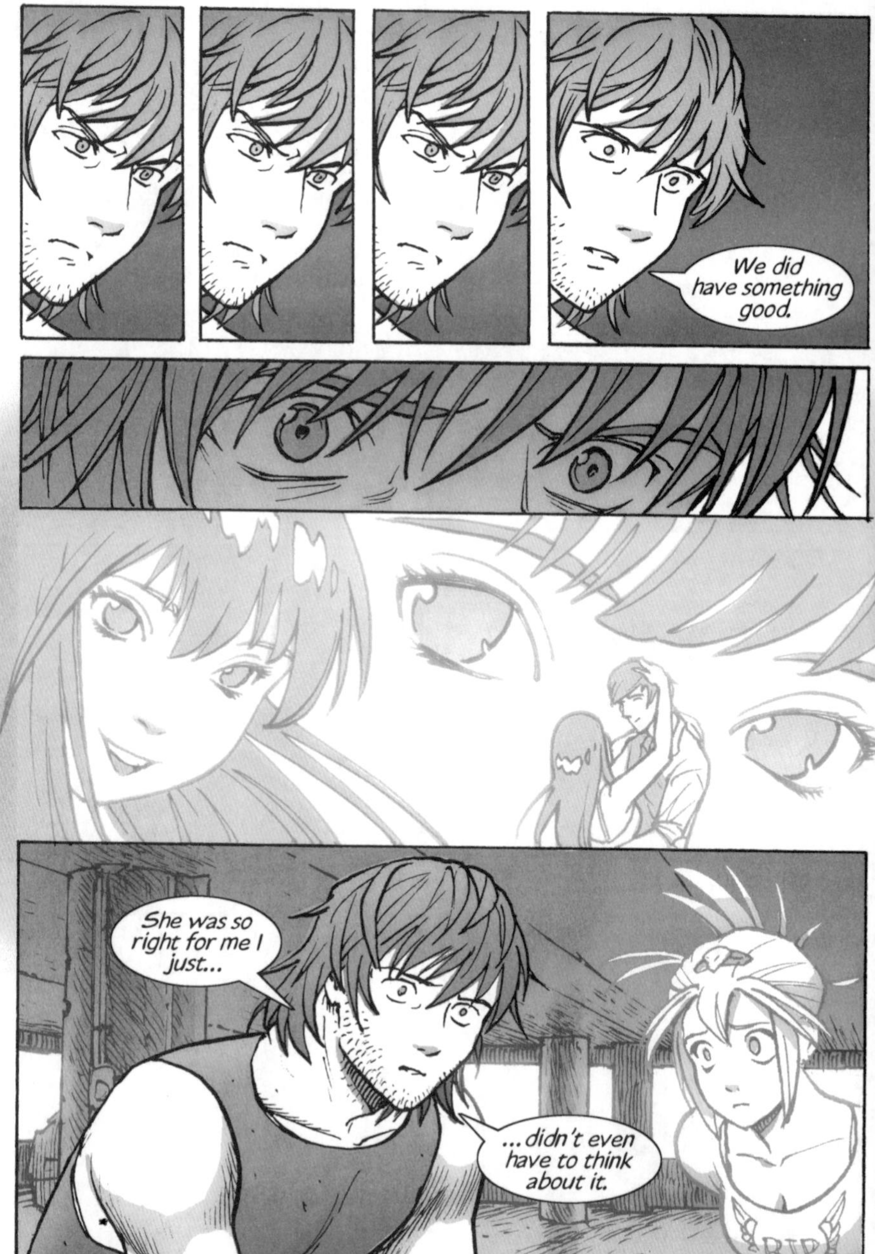
We did have something good.
She was so right for me I just...
...didn't even have to think about it.

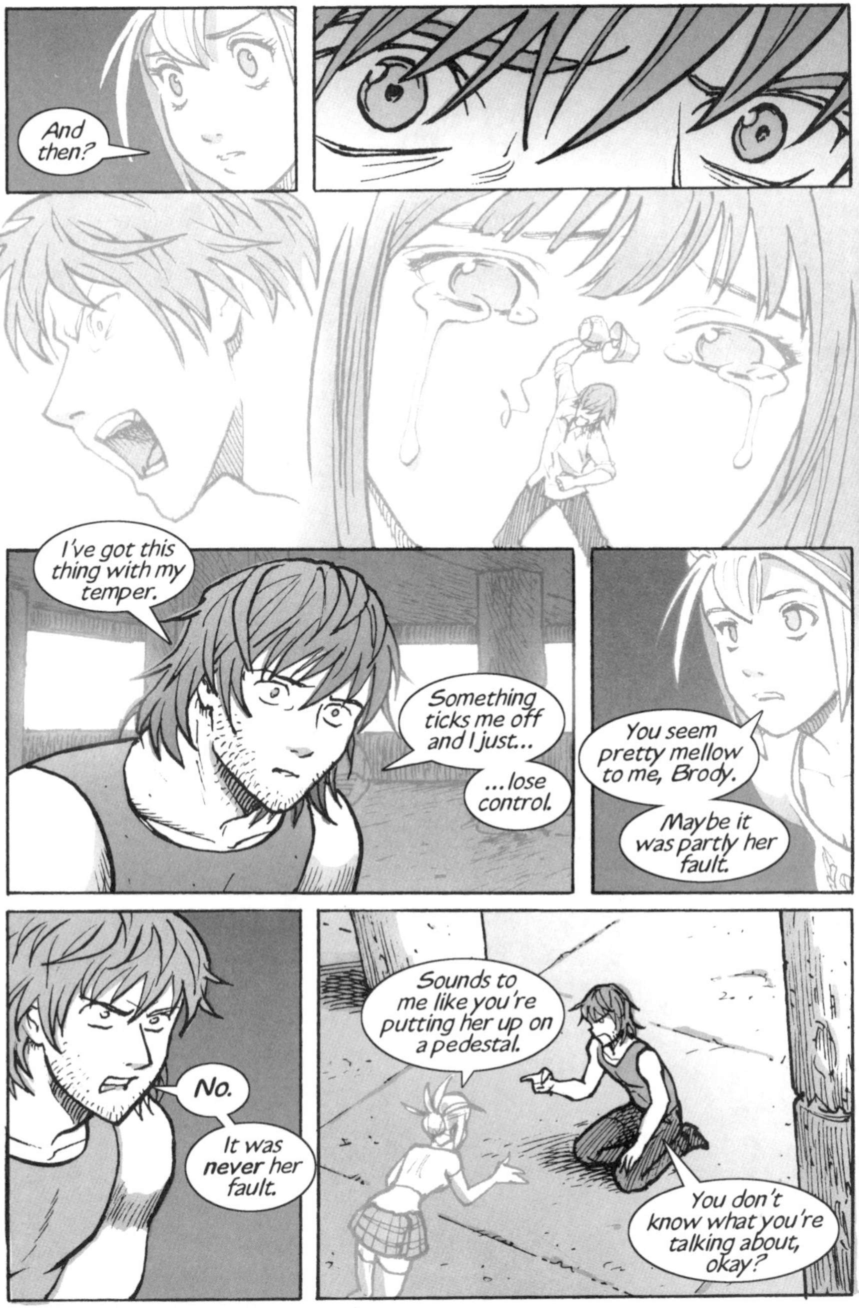
And then?
I've got this thing with my temper.
Something ticks me off and I just...
...lose control.
You seem pretty mellow to me, Brody.
Maybe it was partly her fault.
No.
It was **never** her fault.
Sounds to me like you're putting her up on a pedestal.
You don't know what you're talking about, okay?

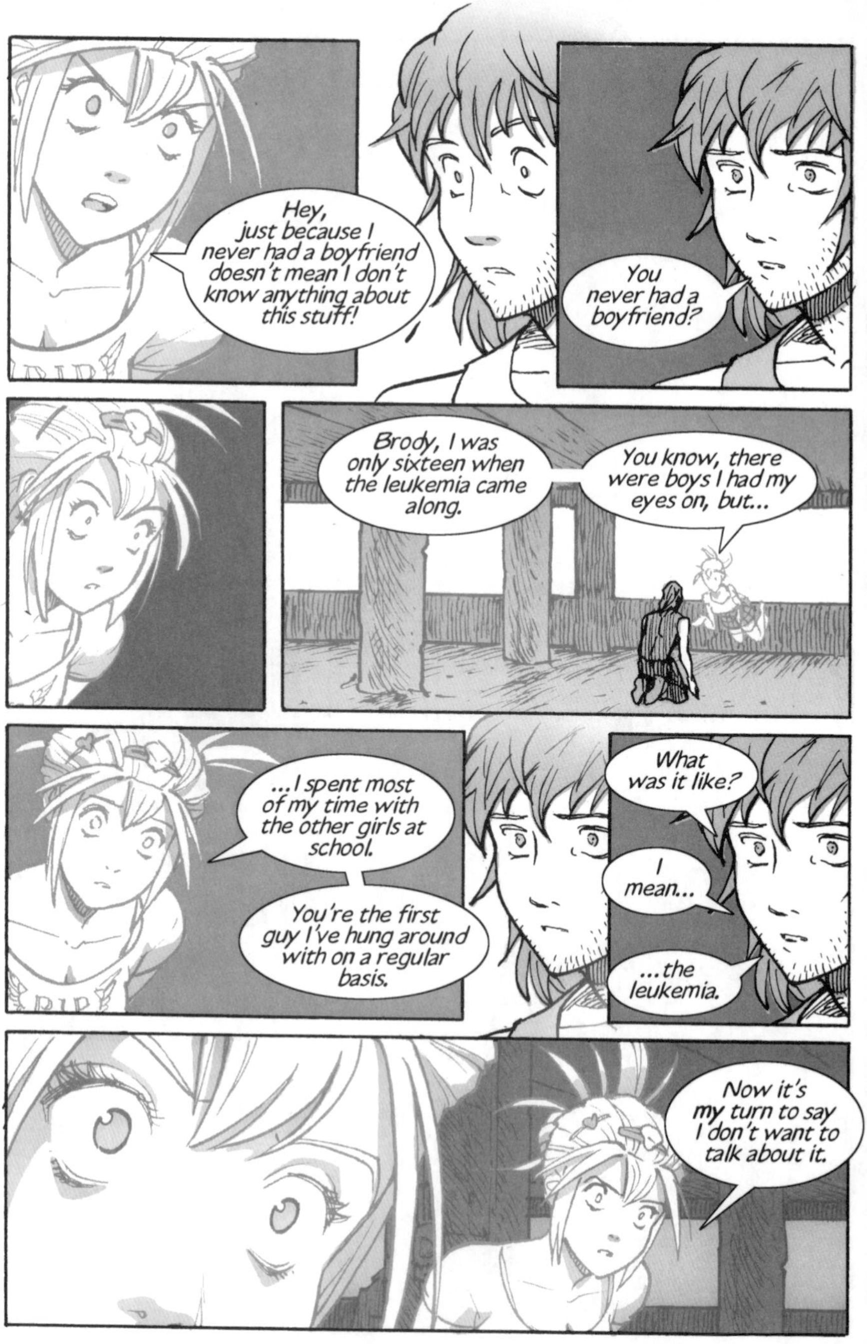
Hey, just because I never had a boyfriend doesn't mean I don't know anything about this stuff!
You never had a boyfriend?
Brody, I was only sixteen when the leukemia came along.
You know, there were boys I had my eyes on, but...
...I spent most of my time with the other girls at school.
You're the first guy I've hung around with on a regular basis.
What was it like?
I mean...
...the leukemia.
Now it's my turn to say I don't want to talk about it.

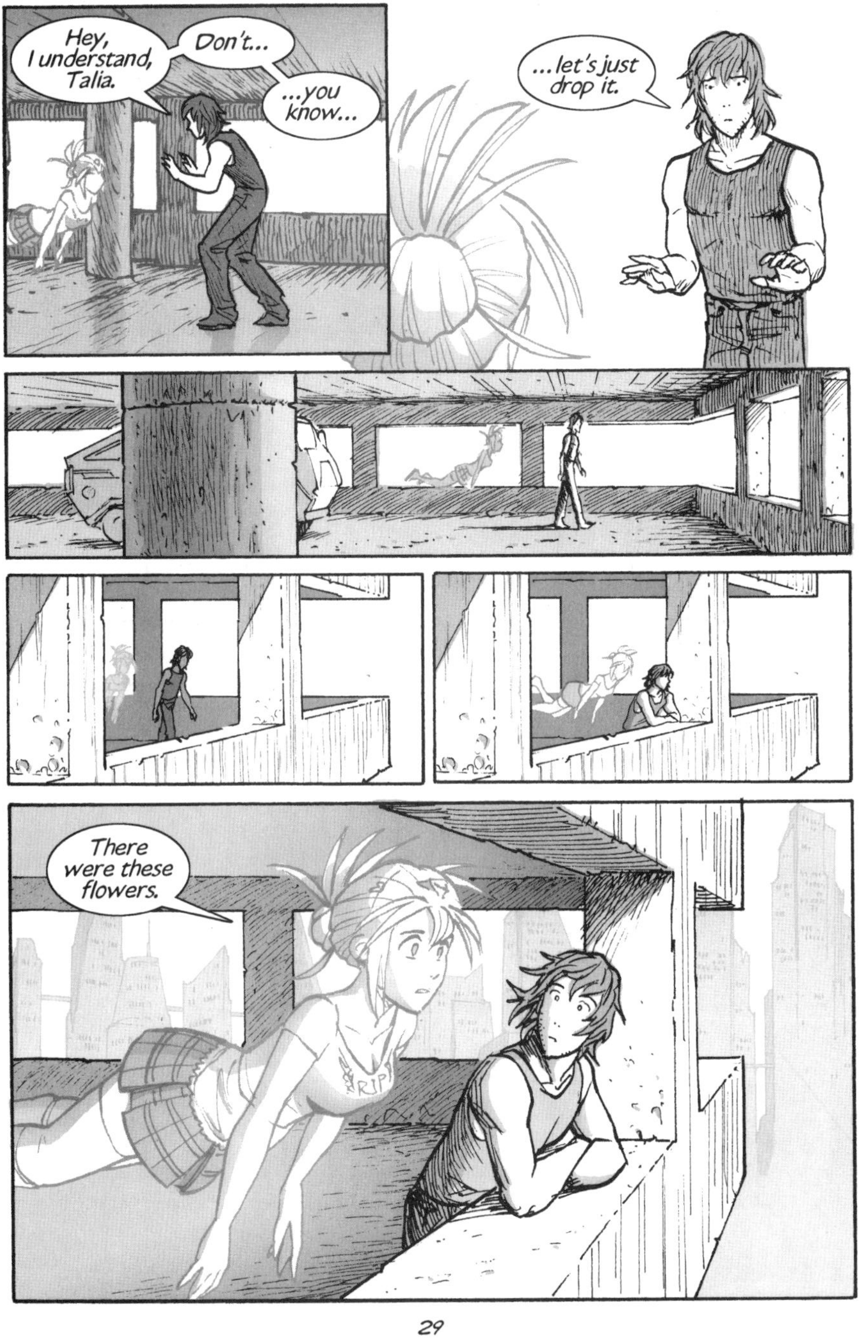
Hey, I understand, Talia.
Don't...
...you know...
...let's just drop it.
There were these flowers.

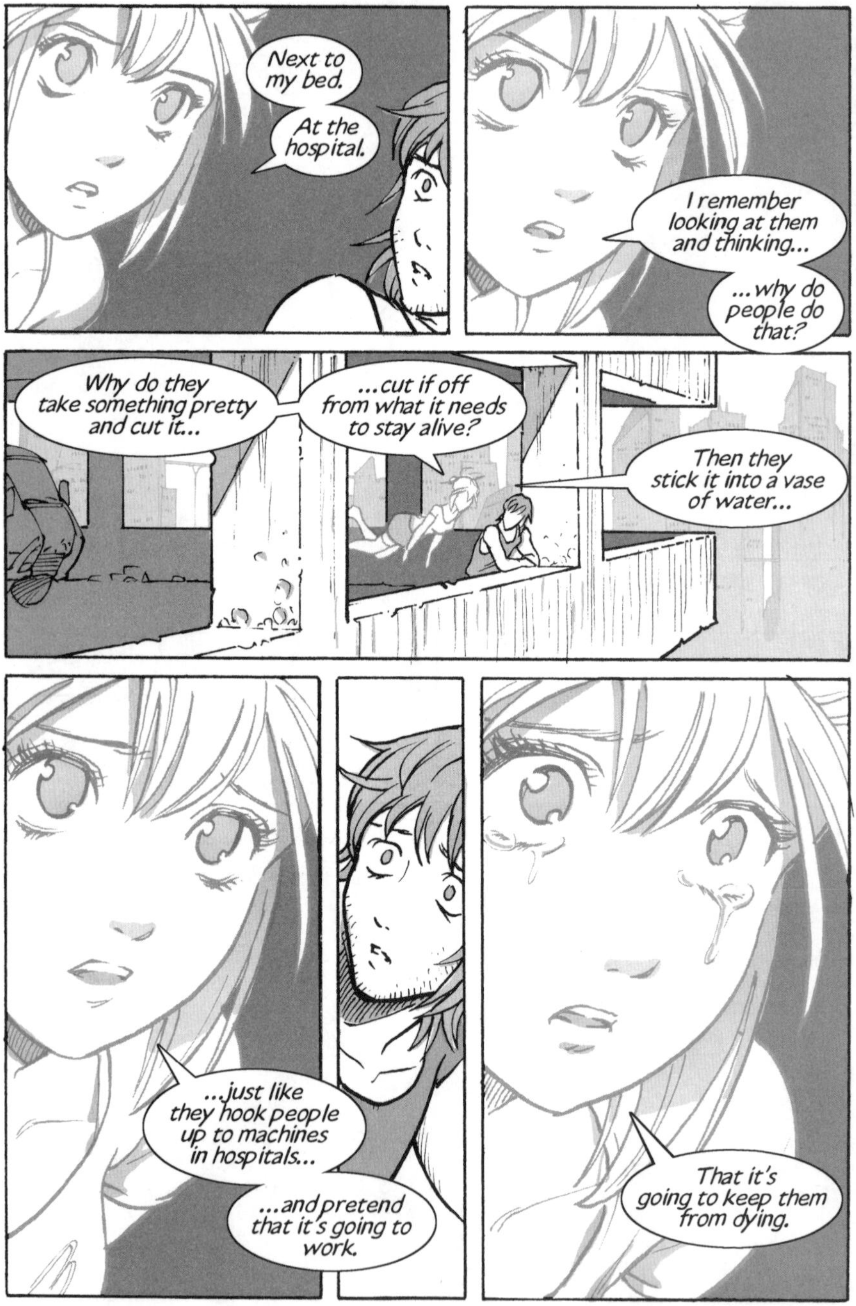
Next to my bed.
At the hospital.
I remember looking at them and thinking...
...why do people do that?
Why do they take something pretty and cut it...
...cut if off from what it needs to stay alive?
Then they stick it into a vase of water...
...just like they hook people up to machines in hospitals...
...and pretend that it's going to work.
That it's going to keep them from dying.

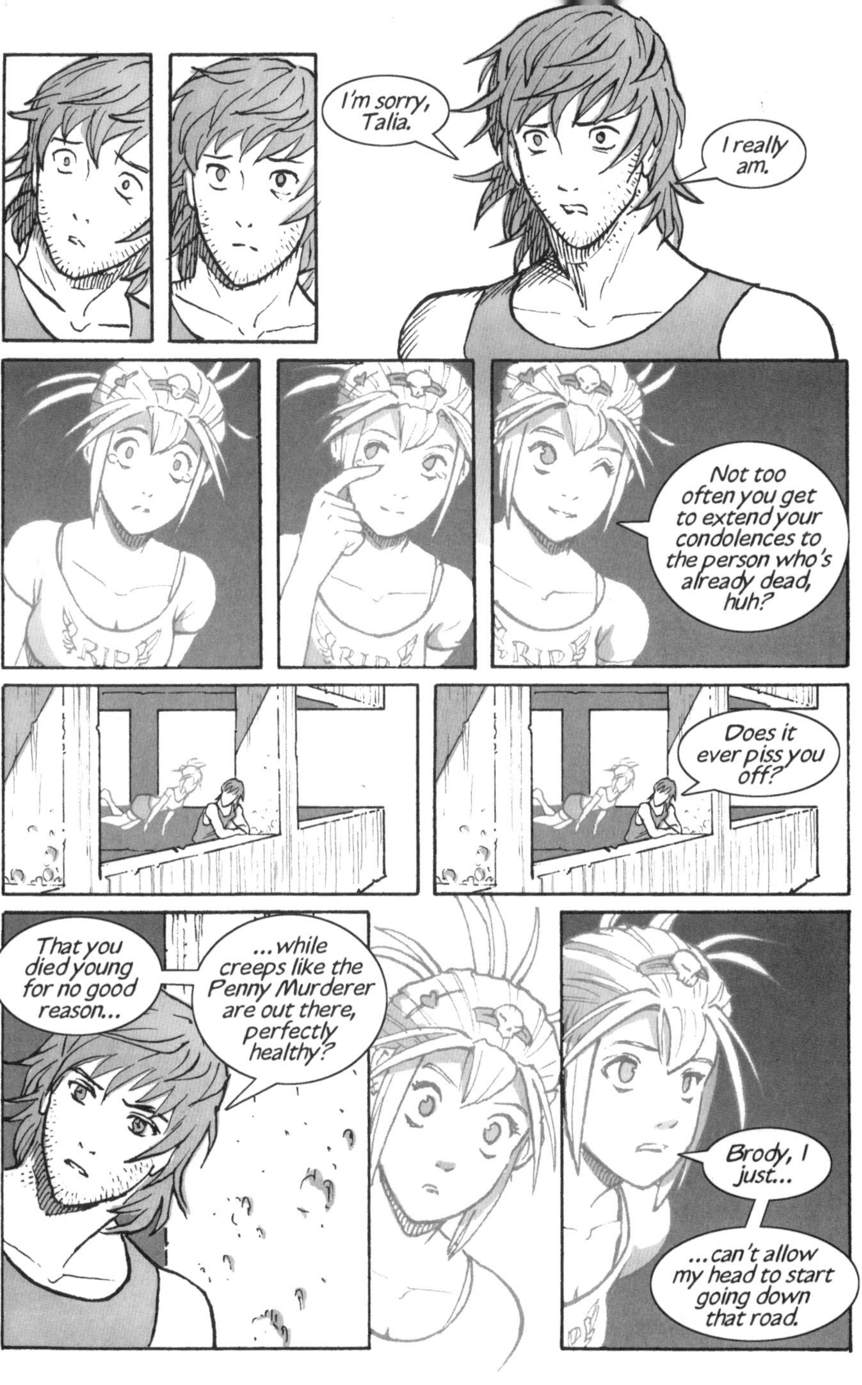
I'm sorry, Talia.
I really am.
Not too often you get to extend your condolences to the person who's already dead, huh?
Does it ever piss you off?
That you died young for no good reason...
...while creeps like the Penny Murderer are out there, perfectly healthy?
Brody, I just...
...can't allow my head to start going down that road.

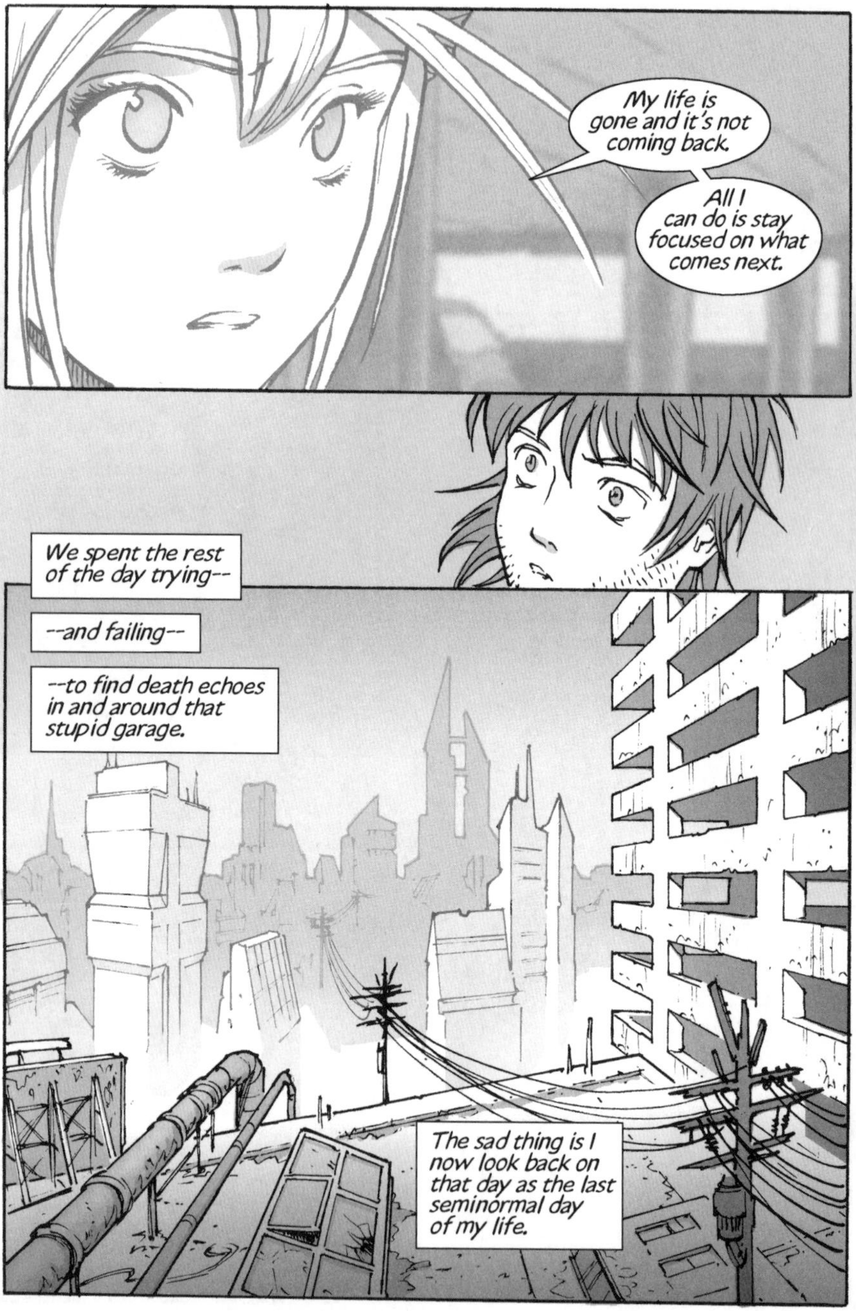
My life is gone and it's not coming back.
All I can do is stay focused on what comes next.
We spent the rest of the day trying--
--and failing--
--to find death echoes in and around that stupid garage.
The sad thing is I now look back on that day as the last seminormal day of my life.

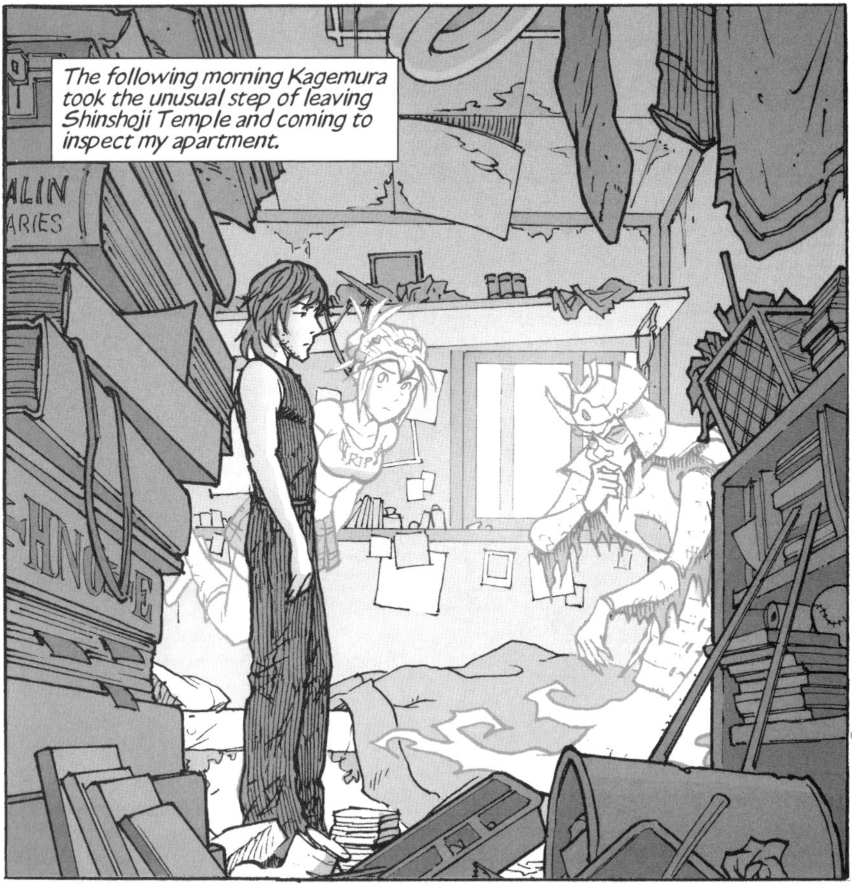
The following morning Kagemura took the unusual step of leaving Shinshoji Temple and coming to inspect my apartment.

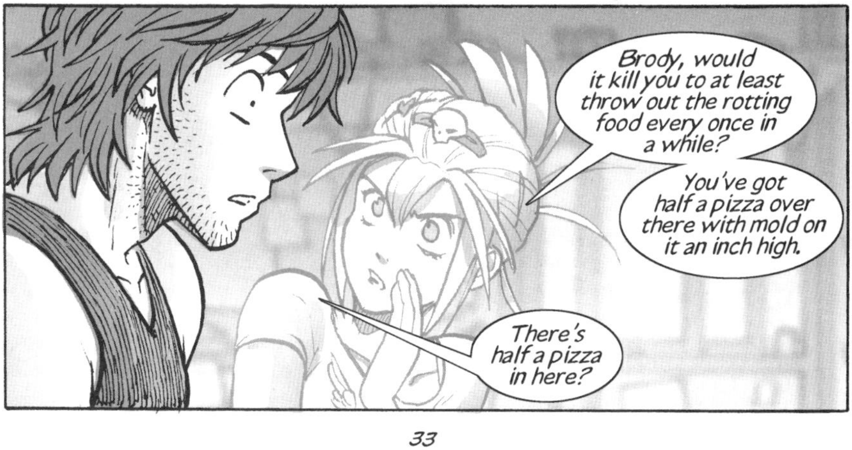
Brody, would it kill you to at least throw out the rotting food every once in a while?
You've got half a pizza over there with mold on it an inch high.
There's half a pizza in here?

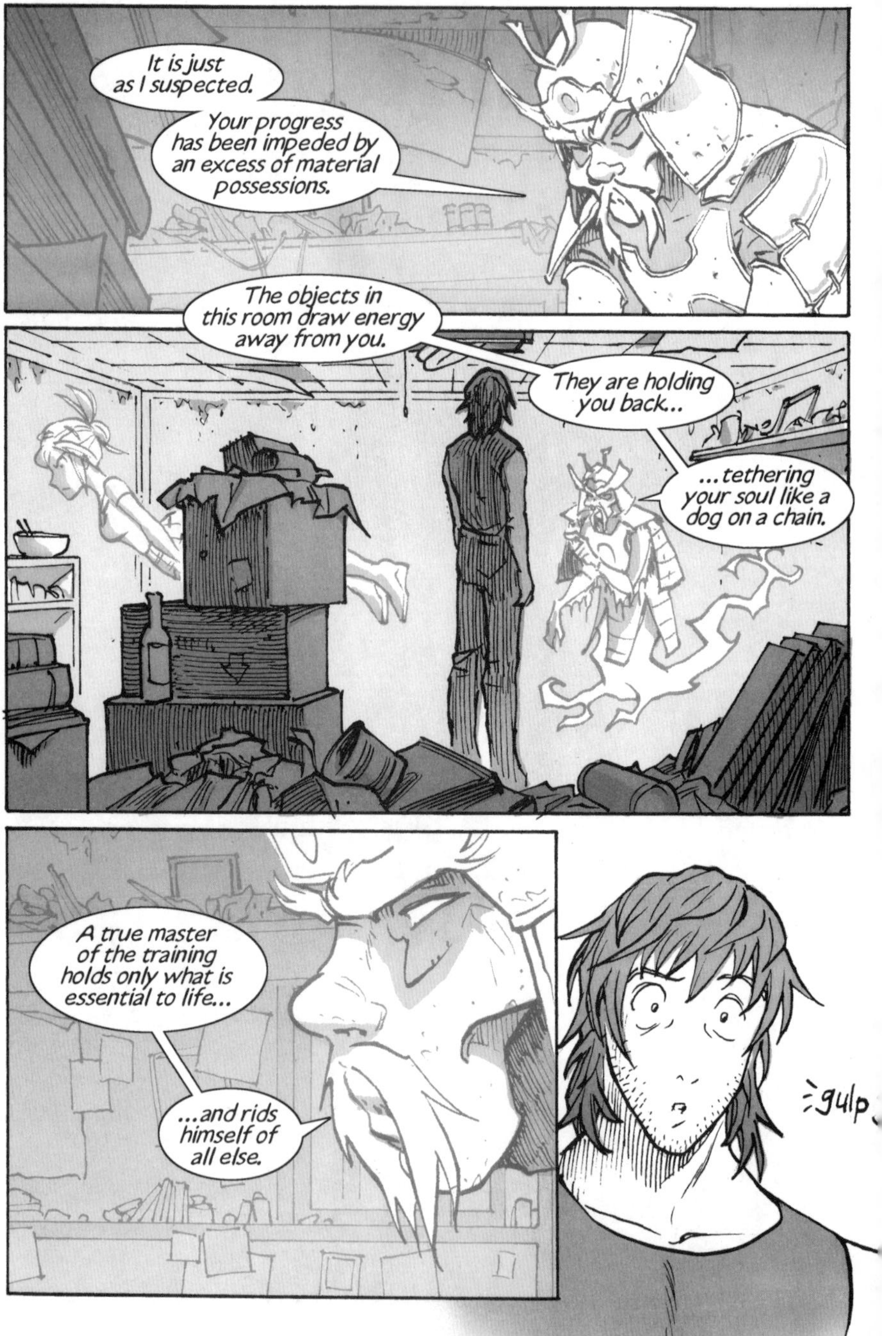
It is just as I suspected.
Your progress has been impeded by an excess of material possessions.
The objects in this room draw energy away from you.
They are holding you back...
...tethering your soul like a dog on a chain.
A true master of the training holds only what is essential to life...
...and rids himself of all else.
gulp

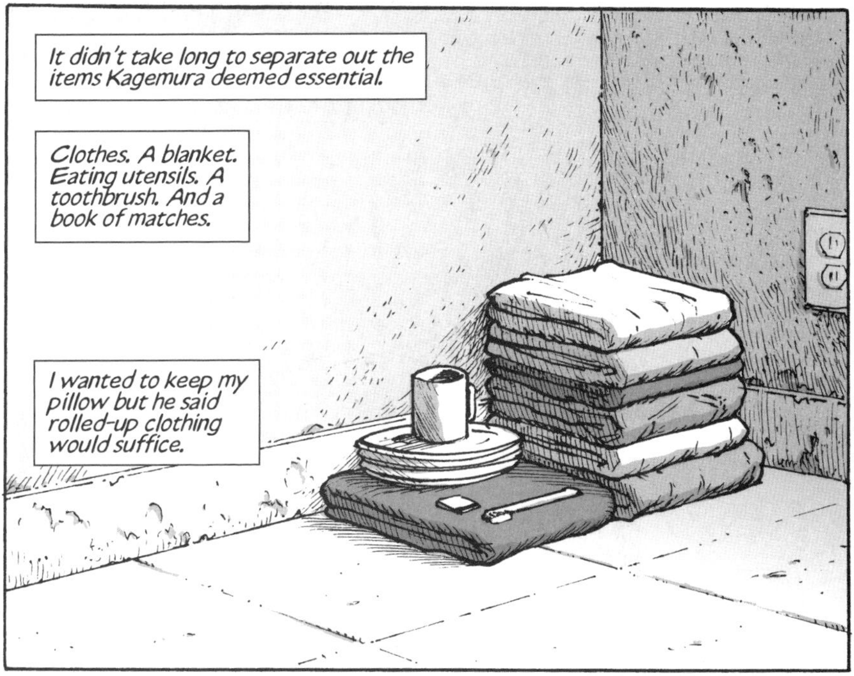
It didn't take long to separate out the items Kagemura deemed essential.
Clothes. A blanket. Eating utensils. A toothbrush. And a book of matches.
I wanted to keep my pillow but he said rolled-up clothing would suffice.

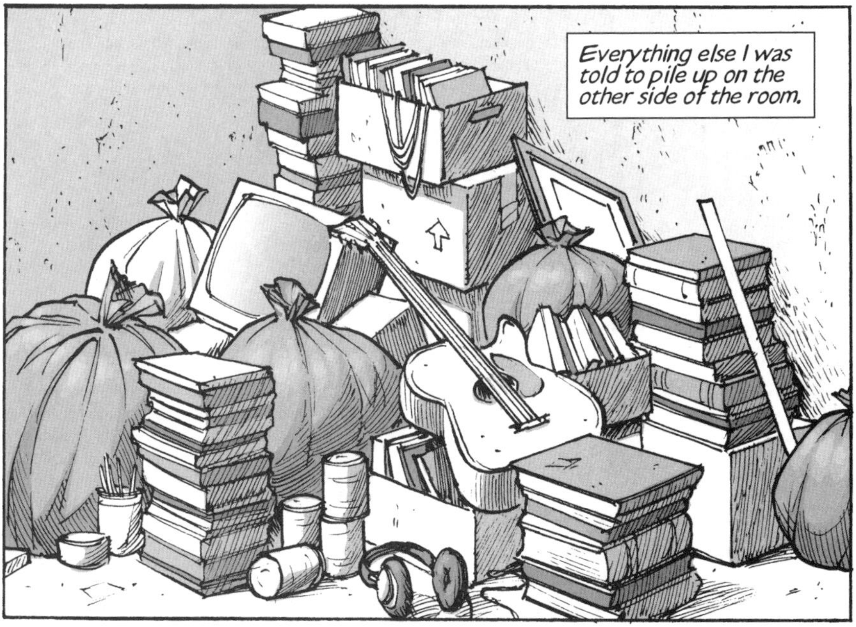
Everything else I was told to pile up on the other side of the room.

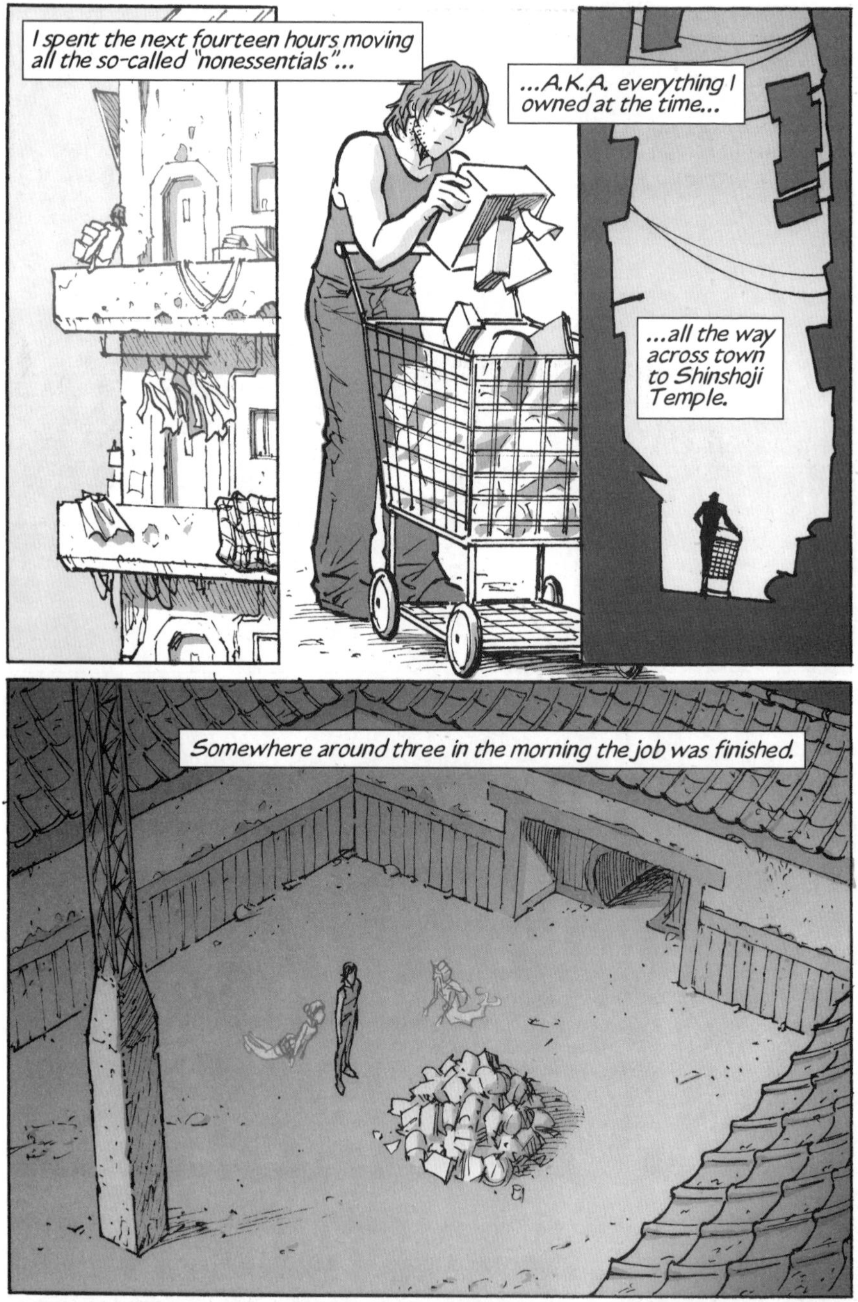
I spent the next fourteen hours moving all the so-called "nonessentials"...
...A.K.A. everything I owned at the time...
...all the way across town to Shinshoji Temple.
Somewhere around three in the morning the job was finished.

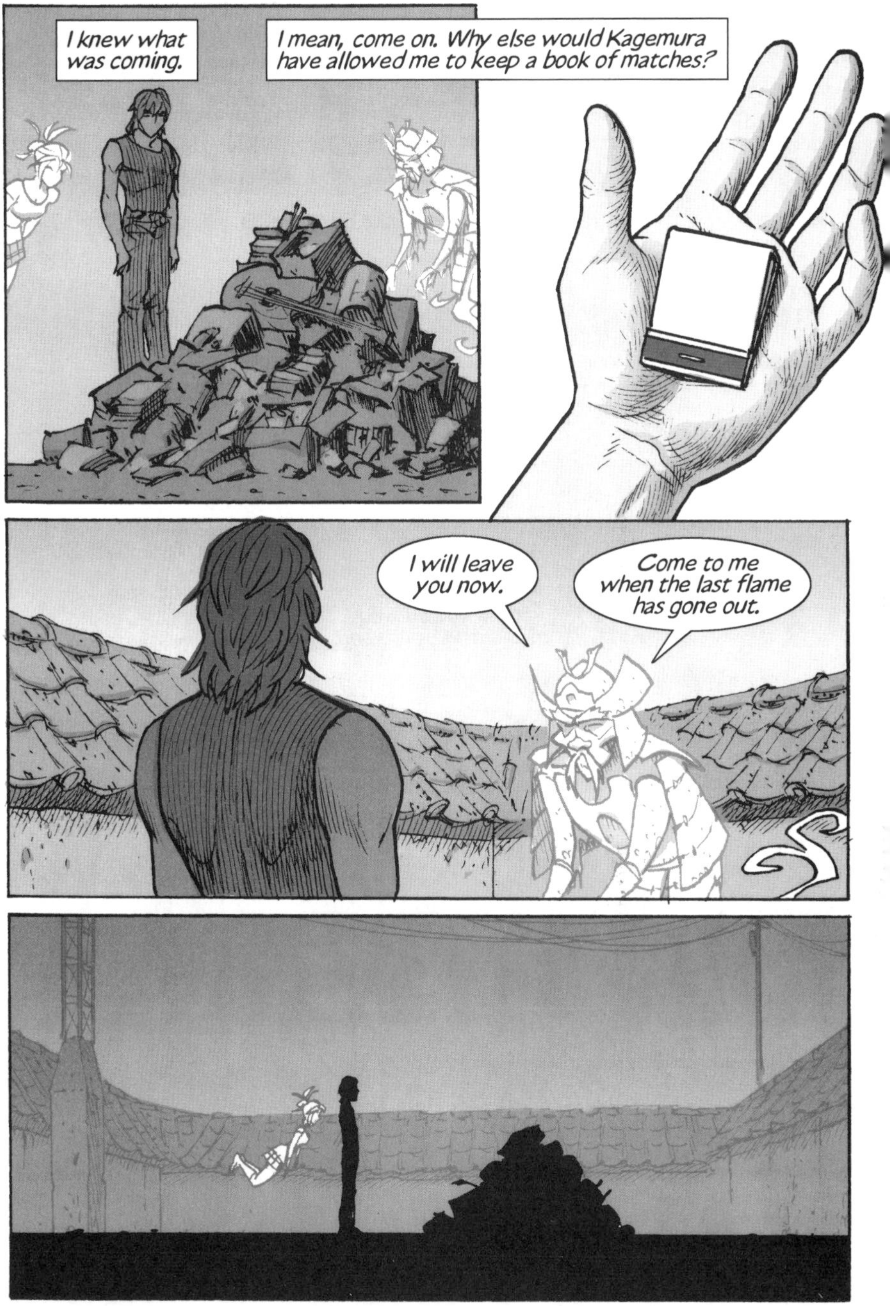
I knew what was coming.
I mean, come on. Why else would Kagemura have allowed me to keep a book of matches?
I will leave you now.
Come to me when the last flame has gone out.

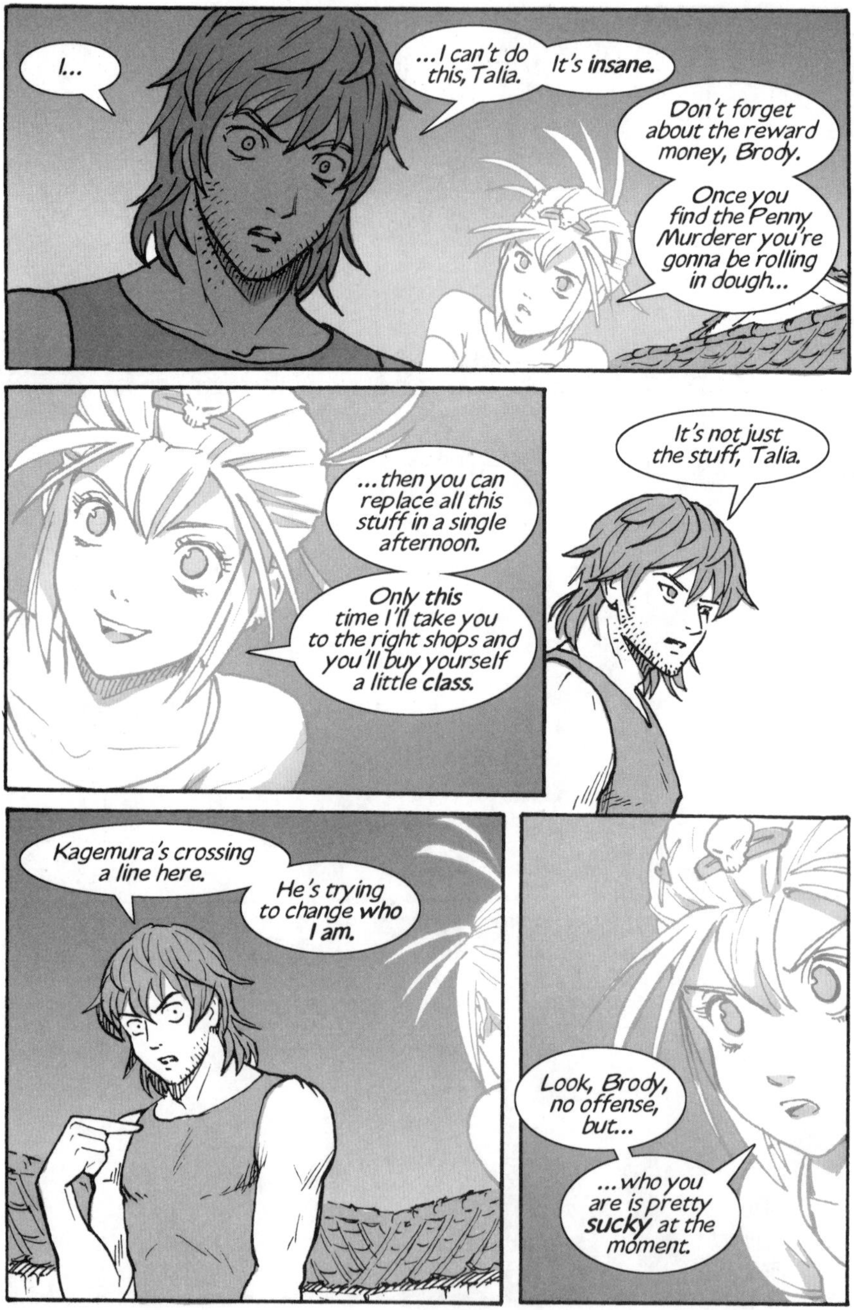
I...
...I can't do this, Talia.
It's insane.
Don't forget about the reward money, Brody.
Once you find the Penny Murderer you're gonna be rolling in dough...
...then you can replace all this stuff in a single afternoon.
Only this time I'll take you to the right shops and you'll buy yourself a little class.
It's not just the stuff, Talia.
Kagemura's crossing a line here.
He's trying to change who I am.
Look, Brody, no offense, but...
...who you are is pretty sucky at the moment.

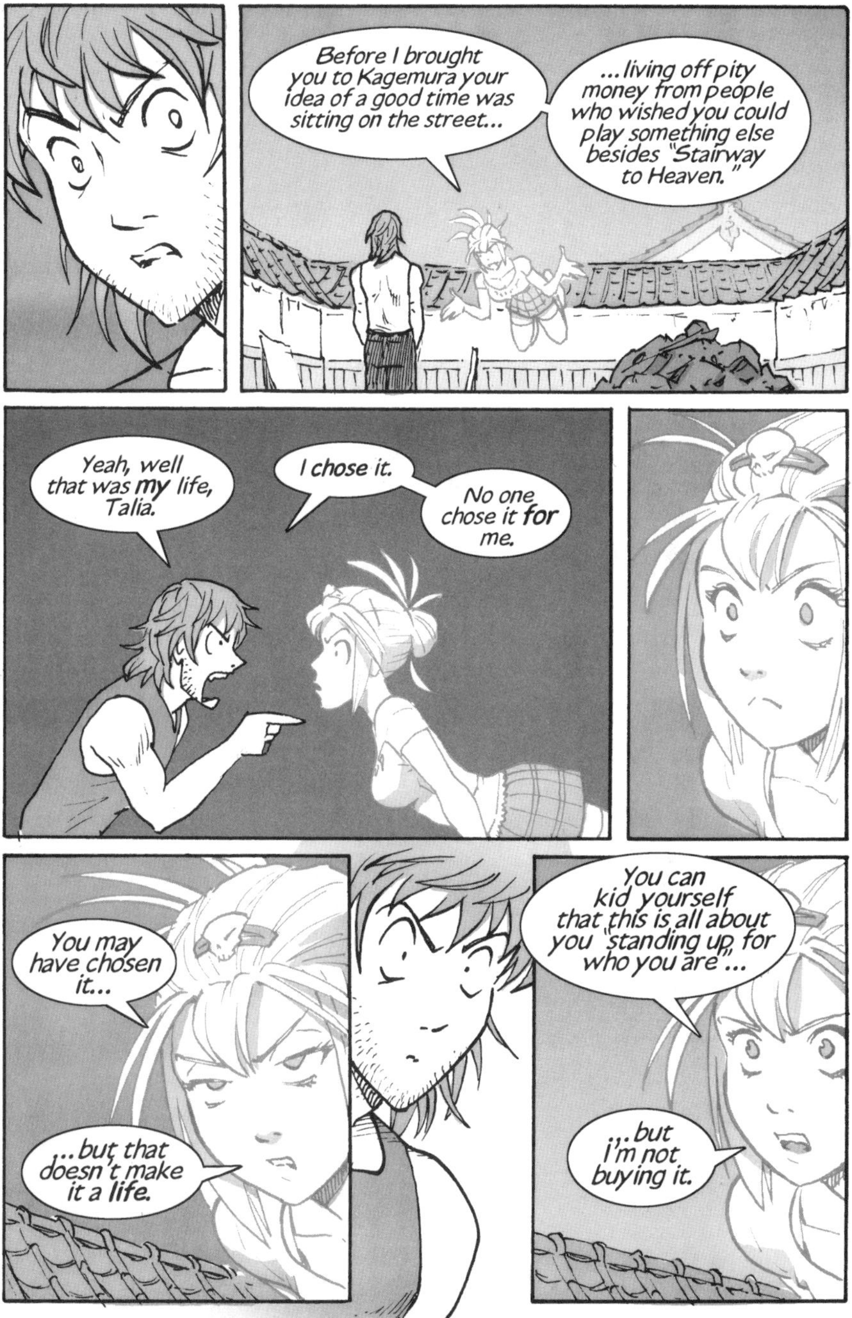
Before I brought you to Kagemura your idea of a good time was sitting on the street...
...living off pity money from people who wished you could play something else besides "Stairway to Heaven."
Yeah, well that was my life, Talia.
I chose it.
No one chose it for me.
You may have chosen it...
...but that doesn't make it a life.
You can kid yourself that this is all about you "standing up for who you are"...
...but I'm not buying it.

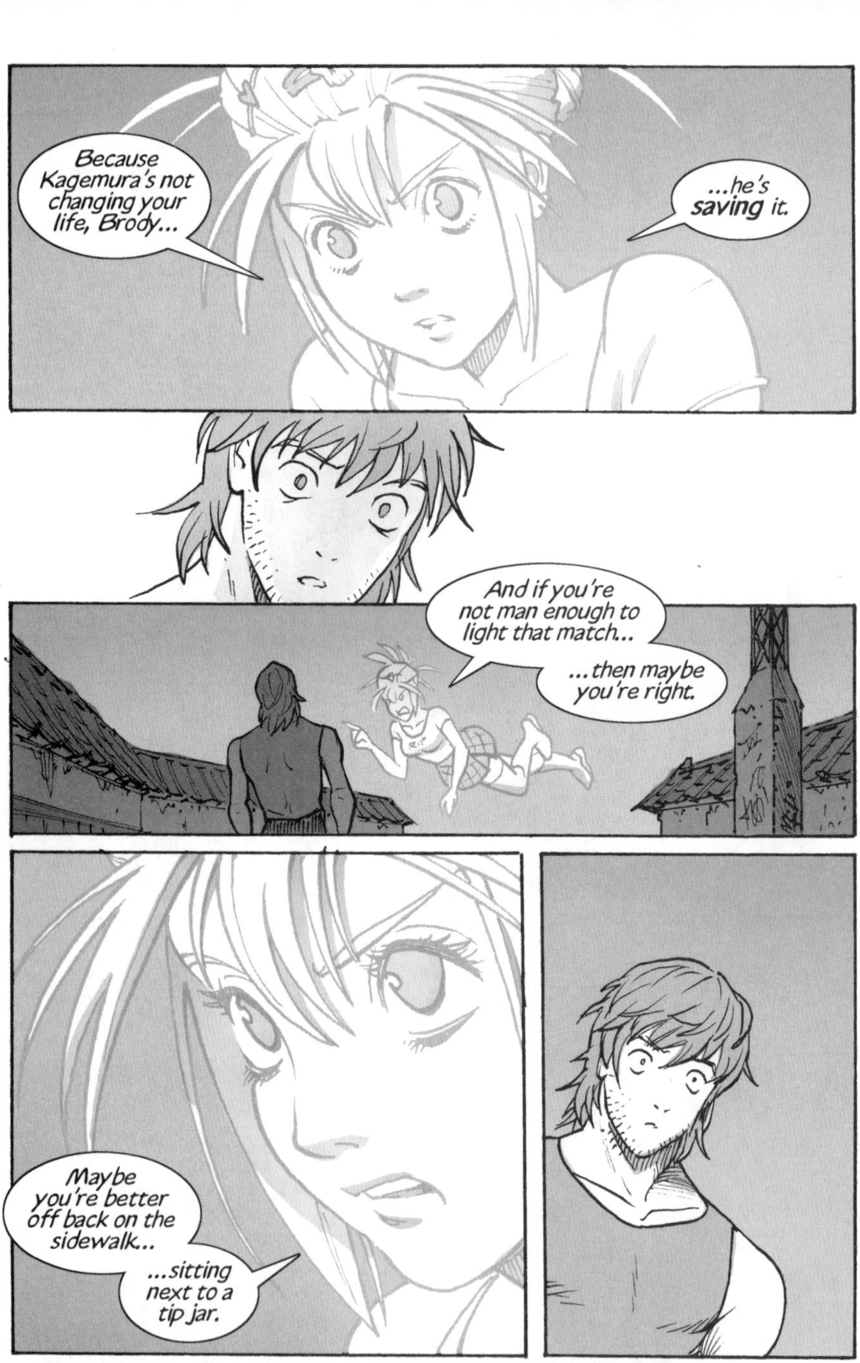
Because Kagemura's not changing your life, Brody...
...he's **saving** it.
And if you're not man enough to light that match...
...then maybe you're right.
Maybe you're better off back on the sidewalk...
...sitting next to a tip jar.

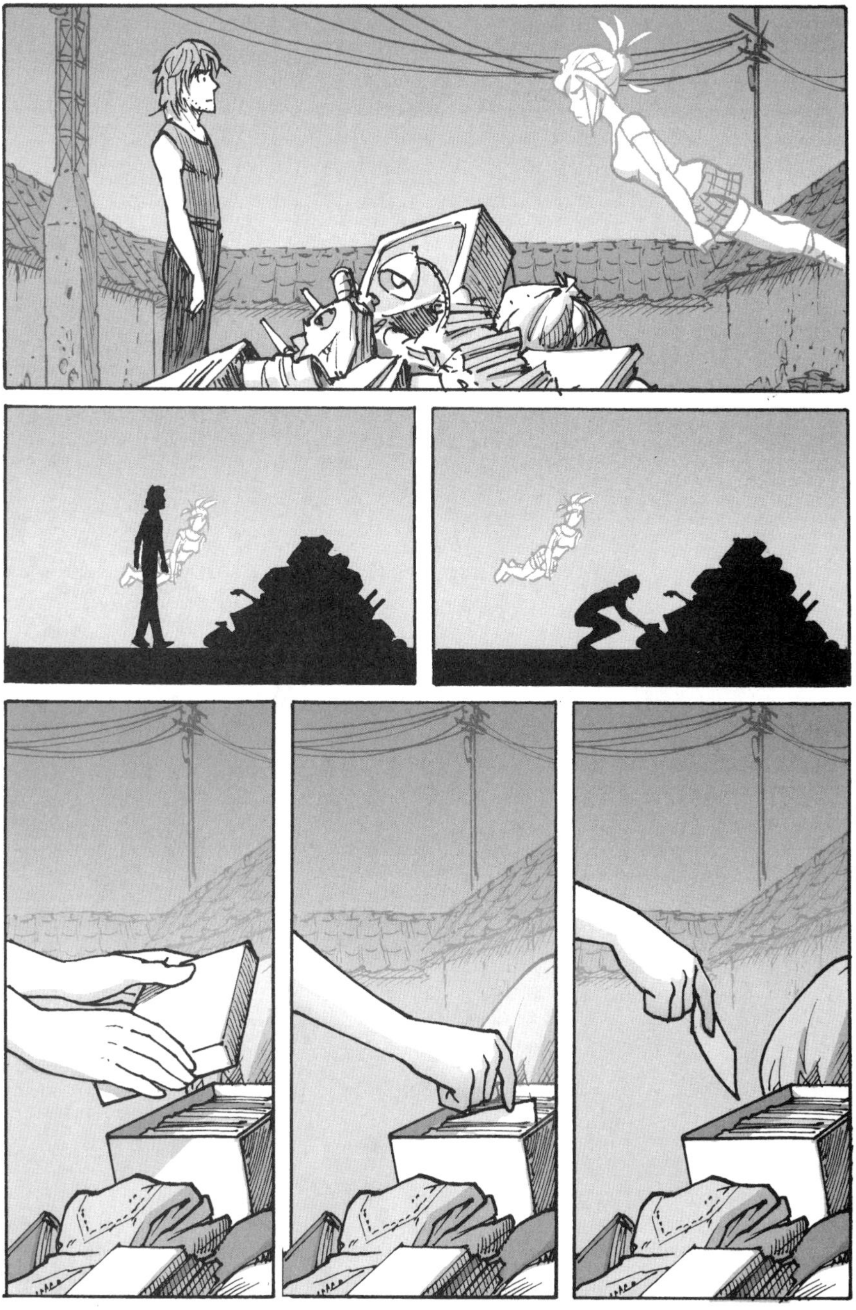

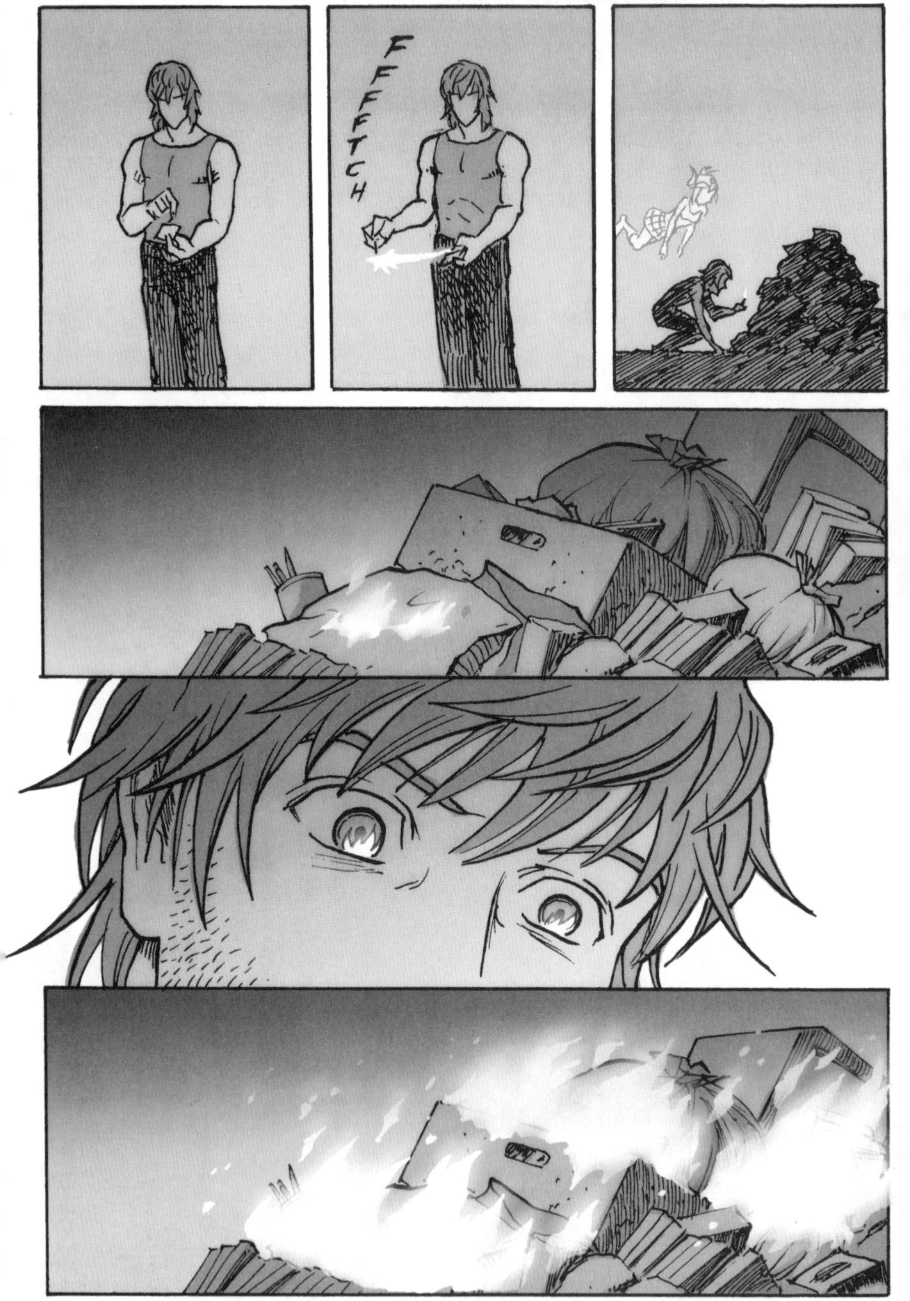
FFFFTCH

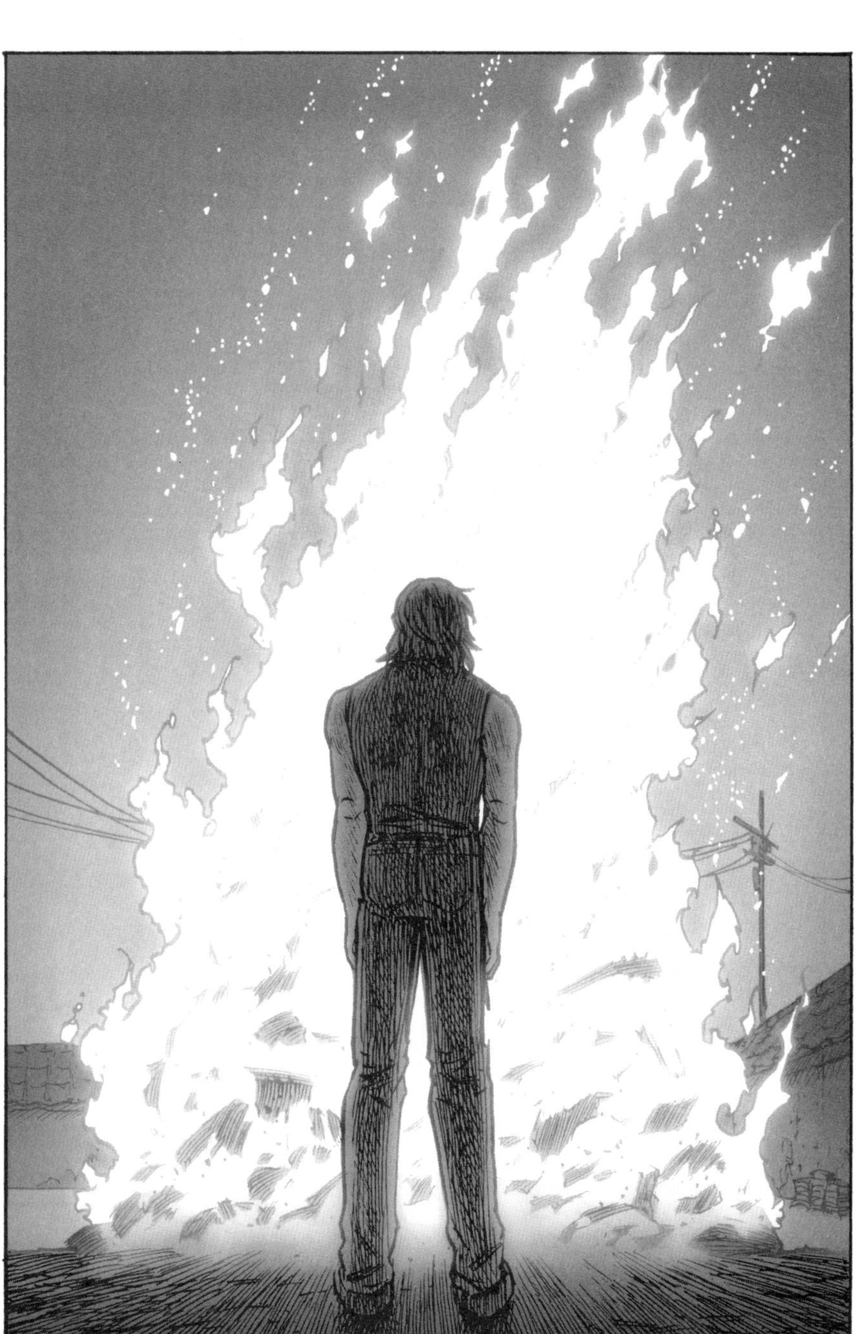

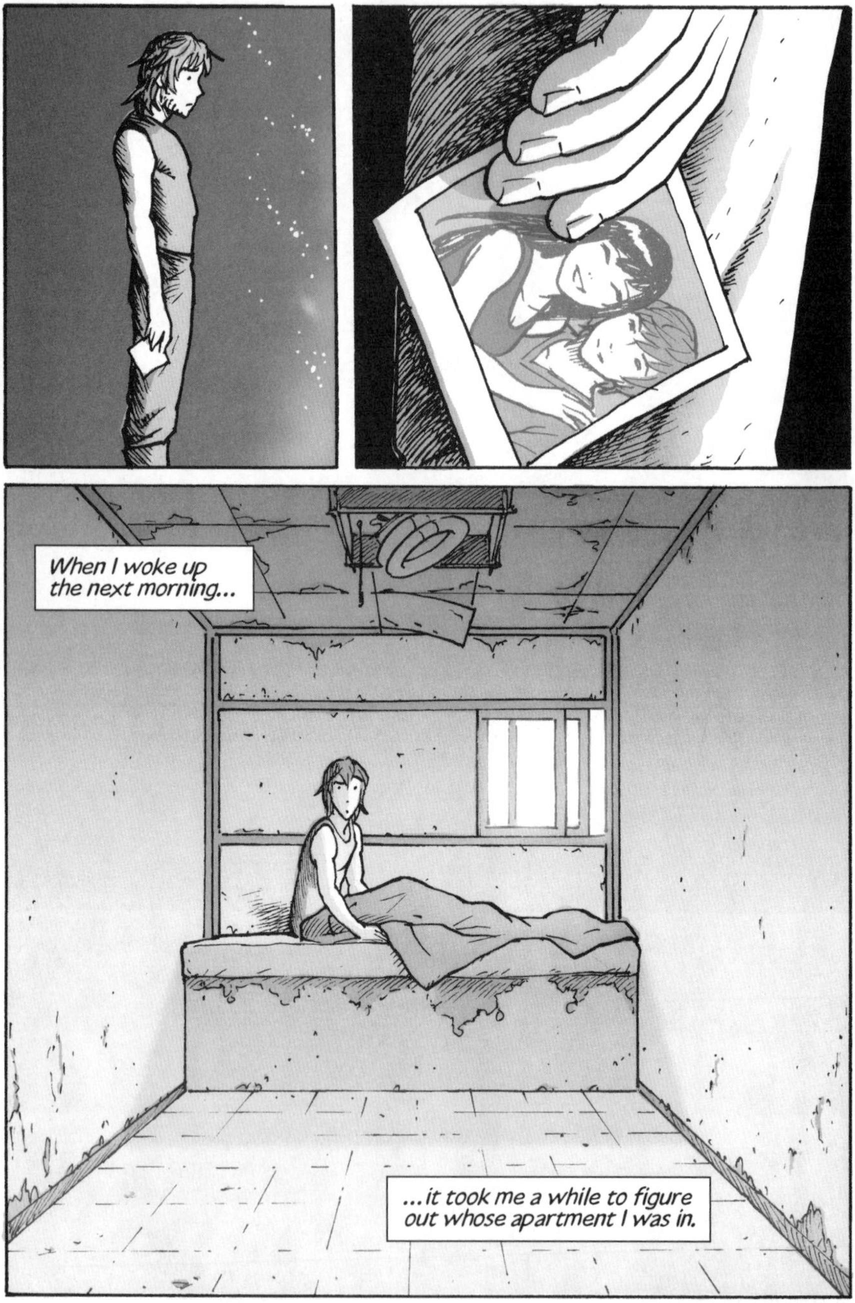
When I woke up the next morning...
...it took me a while to figure out whose apartment I was in.

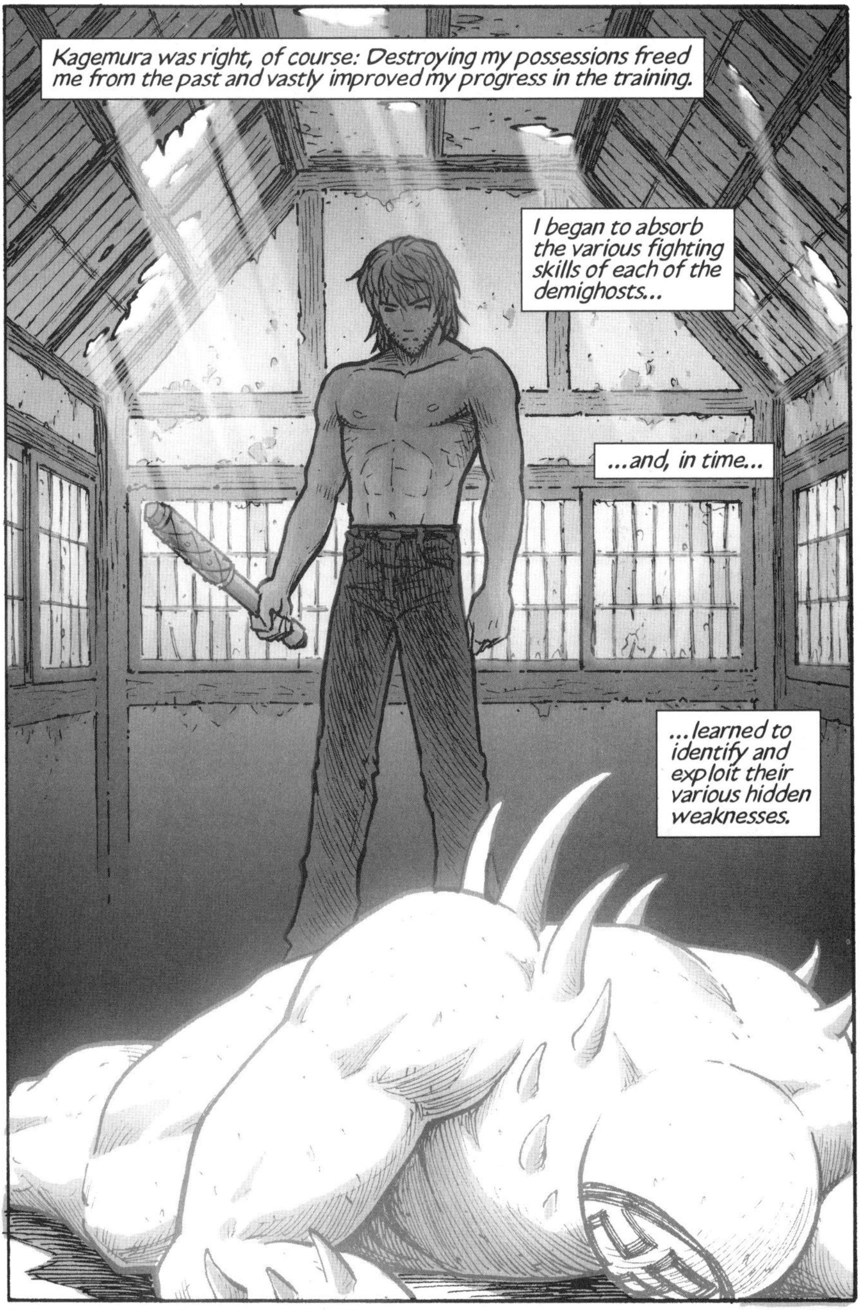
Kagemura was right, of course: Destroying my possessions freed me from the past and vastly improved my progress in the training.
I began to absorb the various fighting skills of each of the demighosts...
...and, in time...
...learned to identify and exploit their various hidden weaknesses.

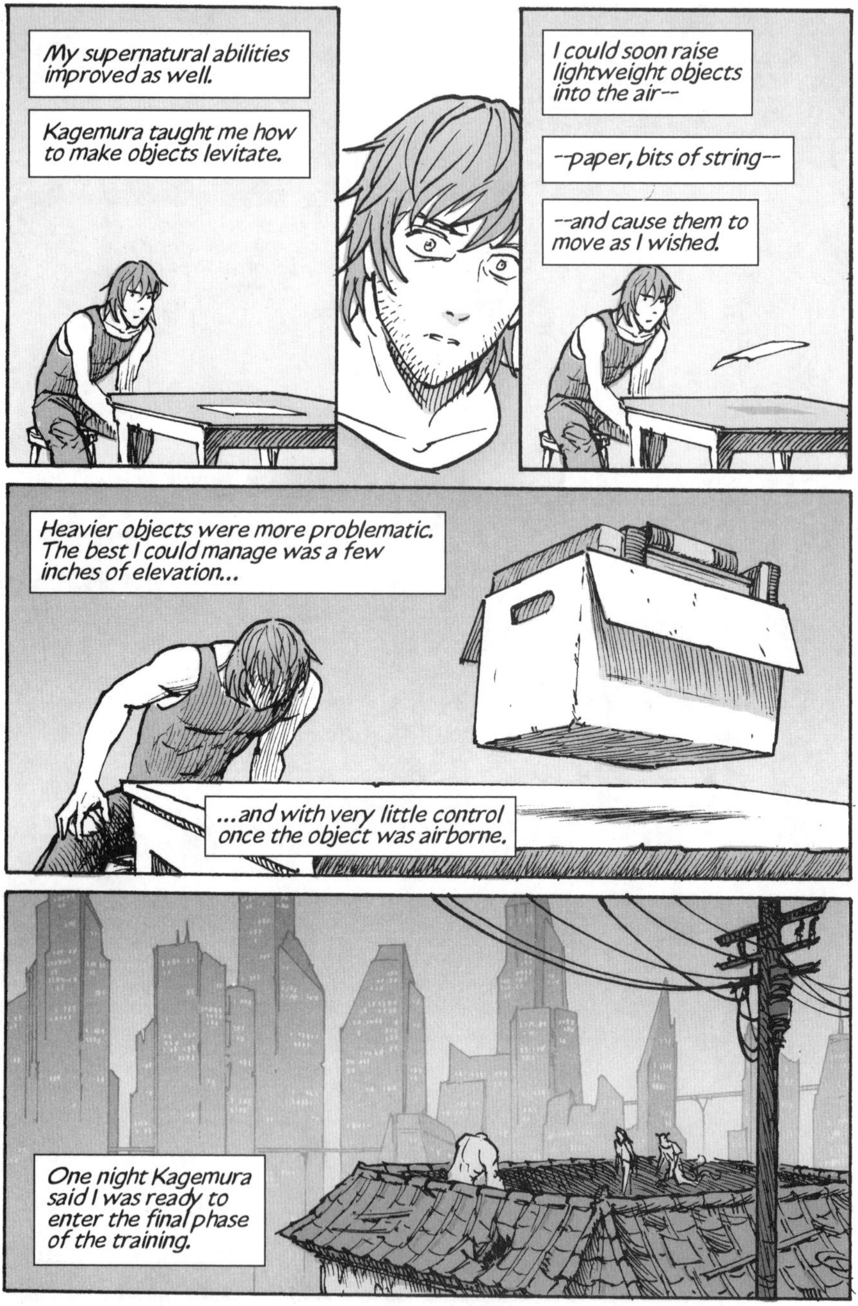
My supernatural abilities improved as well.
Kagemura taught me how to make objects levitate.
I could soon raise lightweight objects into the air--
--paper, bits of string--
--and cause them to move as I wished.
Heavier objects were more problematic. The best I could manage was a few inches of elevation...
...and with very little control once the object was airborne.
One night Kagemura said I was ready to enter the final phase of the training.

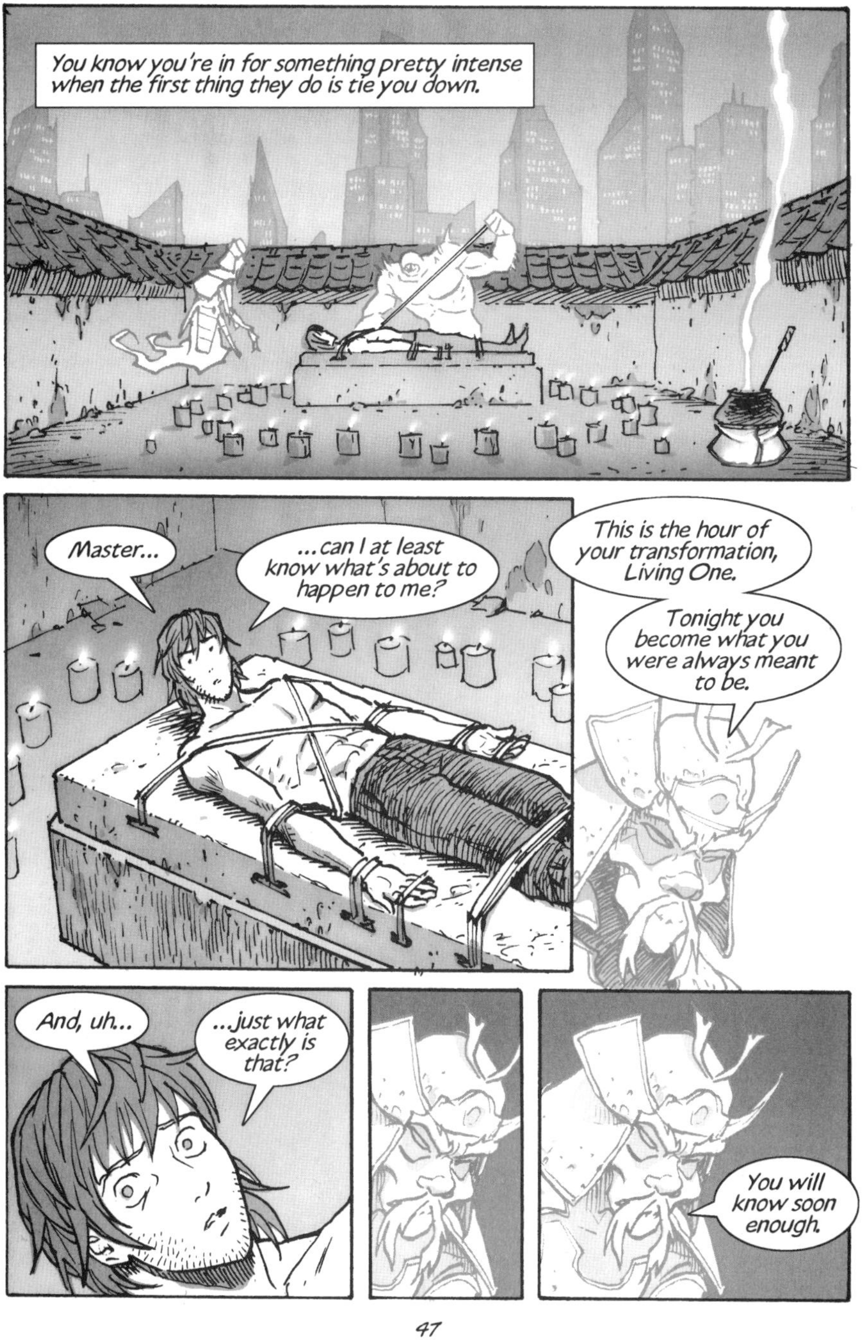
You know you're in for something pretty intense when the first thing they do is tie you down.
Master...
...can I at least know what's about to happen to me?
This is the hour of your transformation, Living One.
Tonight you become what you were always meant to be.
And, uh...
...just what exactly is that?
You will know soon enough.

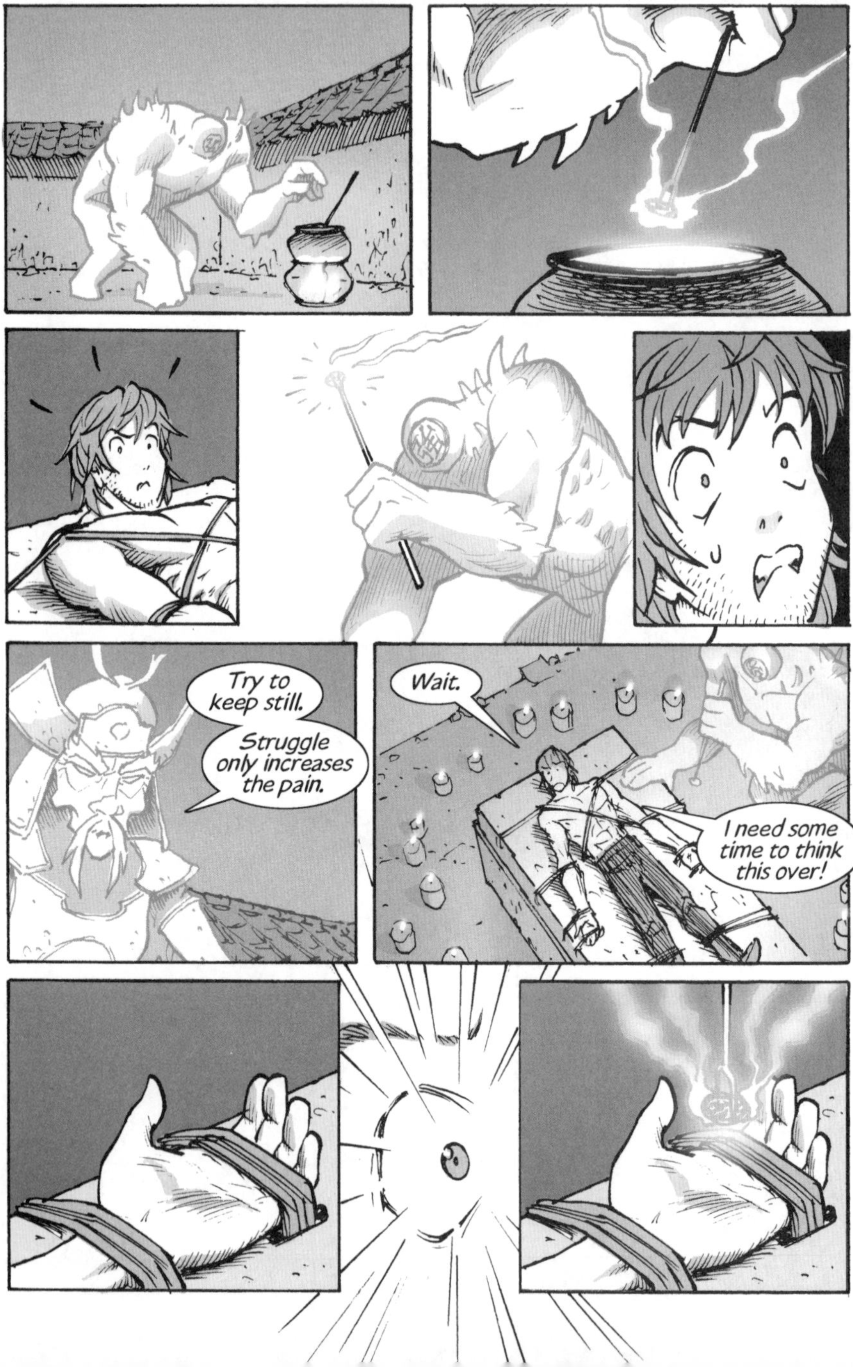
Try to keep still.
Struggle only increases the pain.
Wait.
I need some time to think this over!

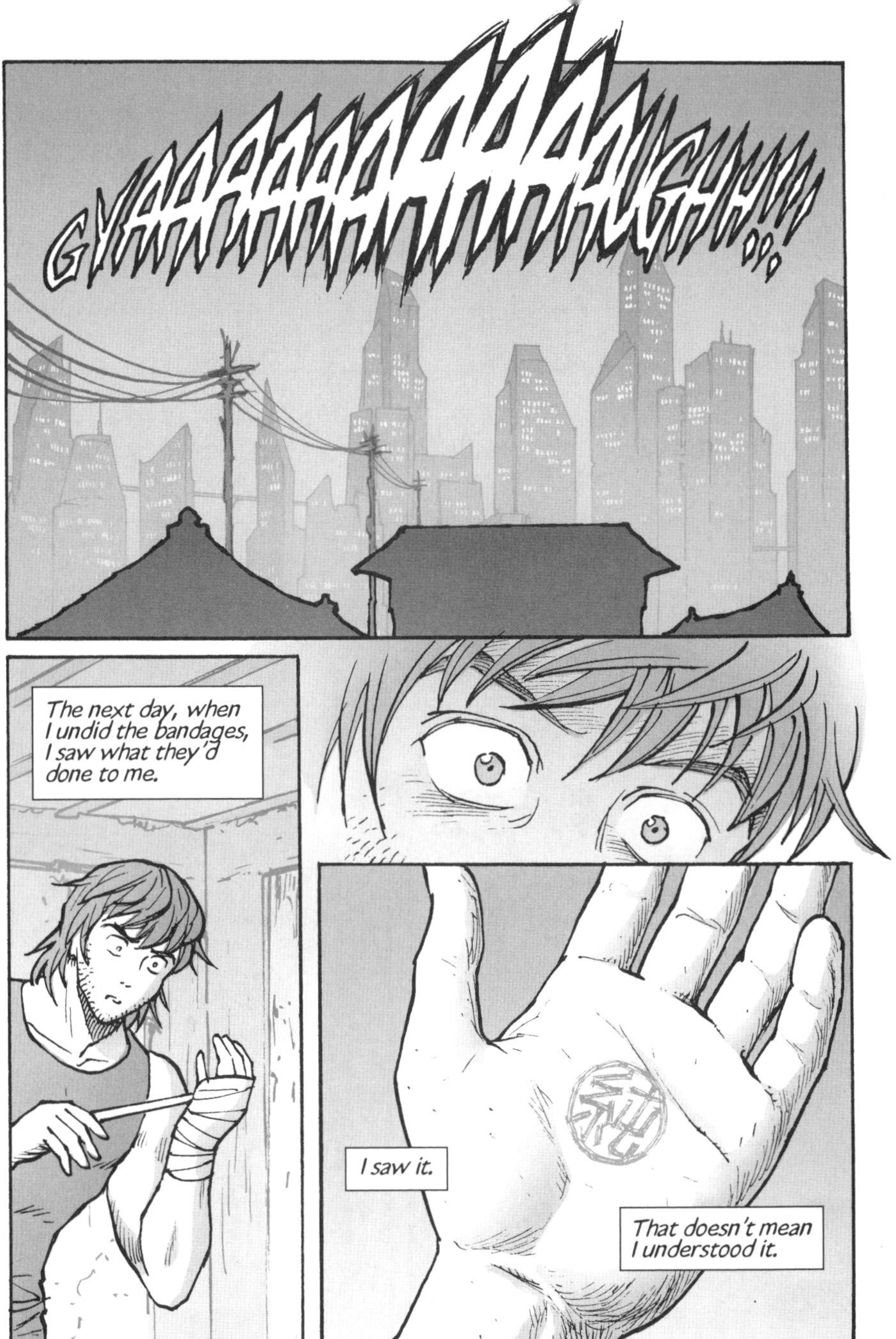
GYAAAAAAAAAAAAAAAAAAAAGH!!!
The next day, when I undid the bandages, I saw what they'd done to me.
I saw it.
That doesn't mean I understood it.

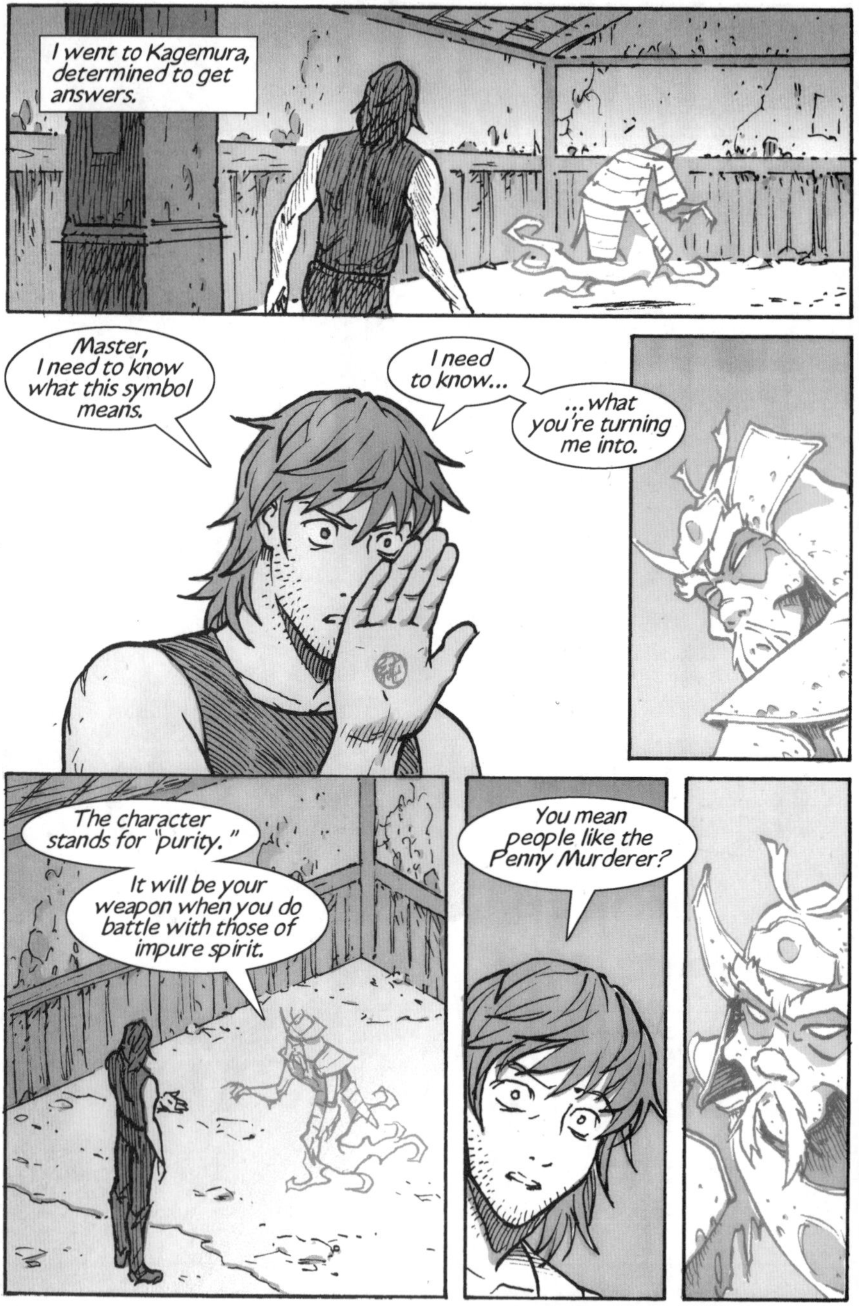
I went to Kagemura, determined to get answers.
Master, I need to know what this symbol means.
I need to know...
...what you're turning me into.
The character stands for "purity."
It will be your weapon when you do battle with those of impure spirit.
You mean people like the Penny Murderer?

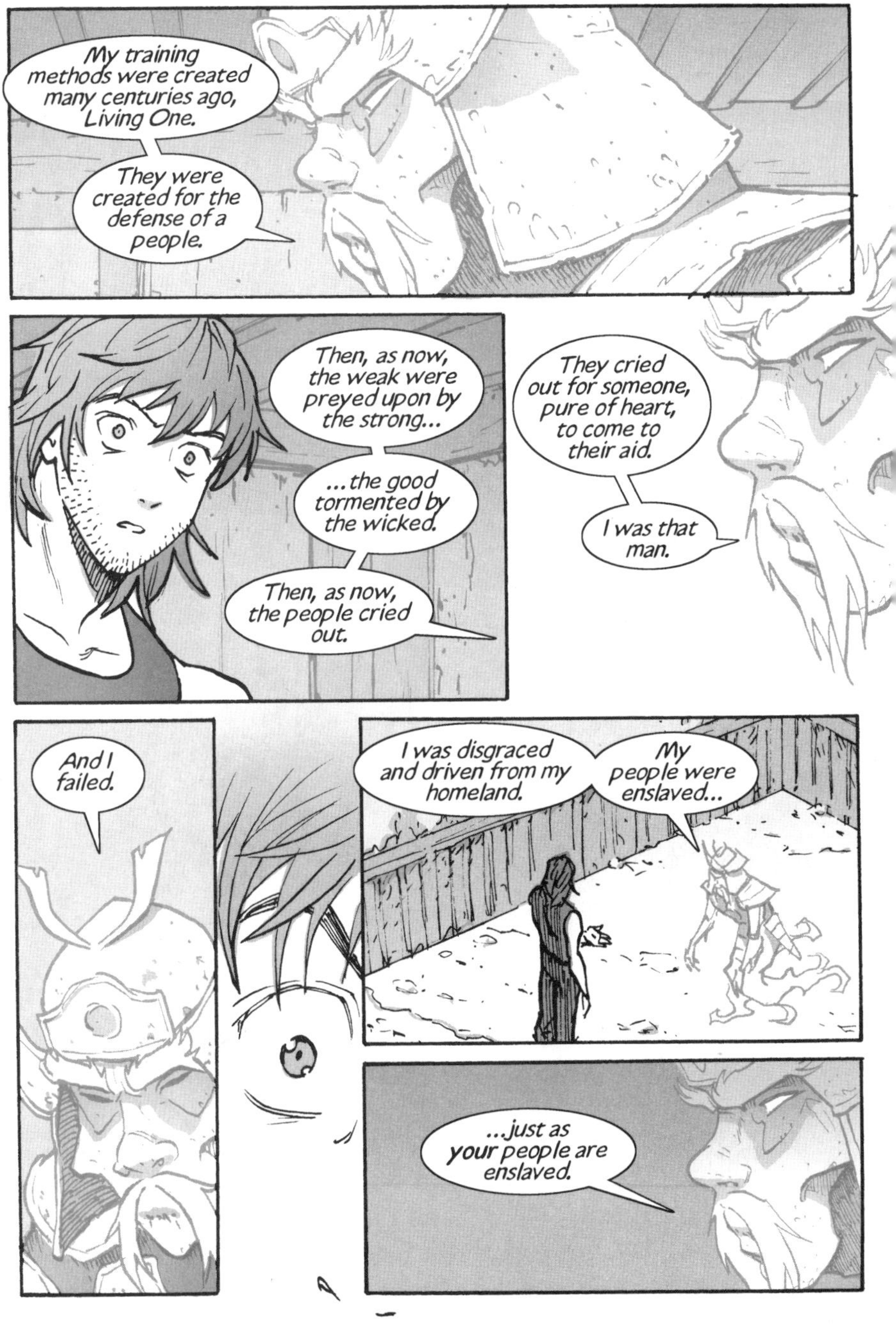
My training methods were created many centuries ago, Living One.
They were created for the defense of a people.
Then, as now, the weak were preyed upon by the strong...
...the good tormented by the wicked.
Then, as now, the people cried out.
They cried out for someone, pure of heart, to come to their aid.
I was that man.
And I failed.
I was disgraced and driven from my homeland.
My people were enslaved...
...just as your people are enslaved.

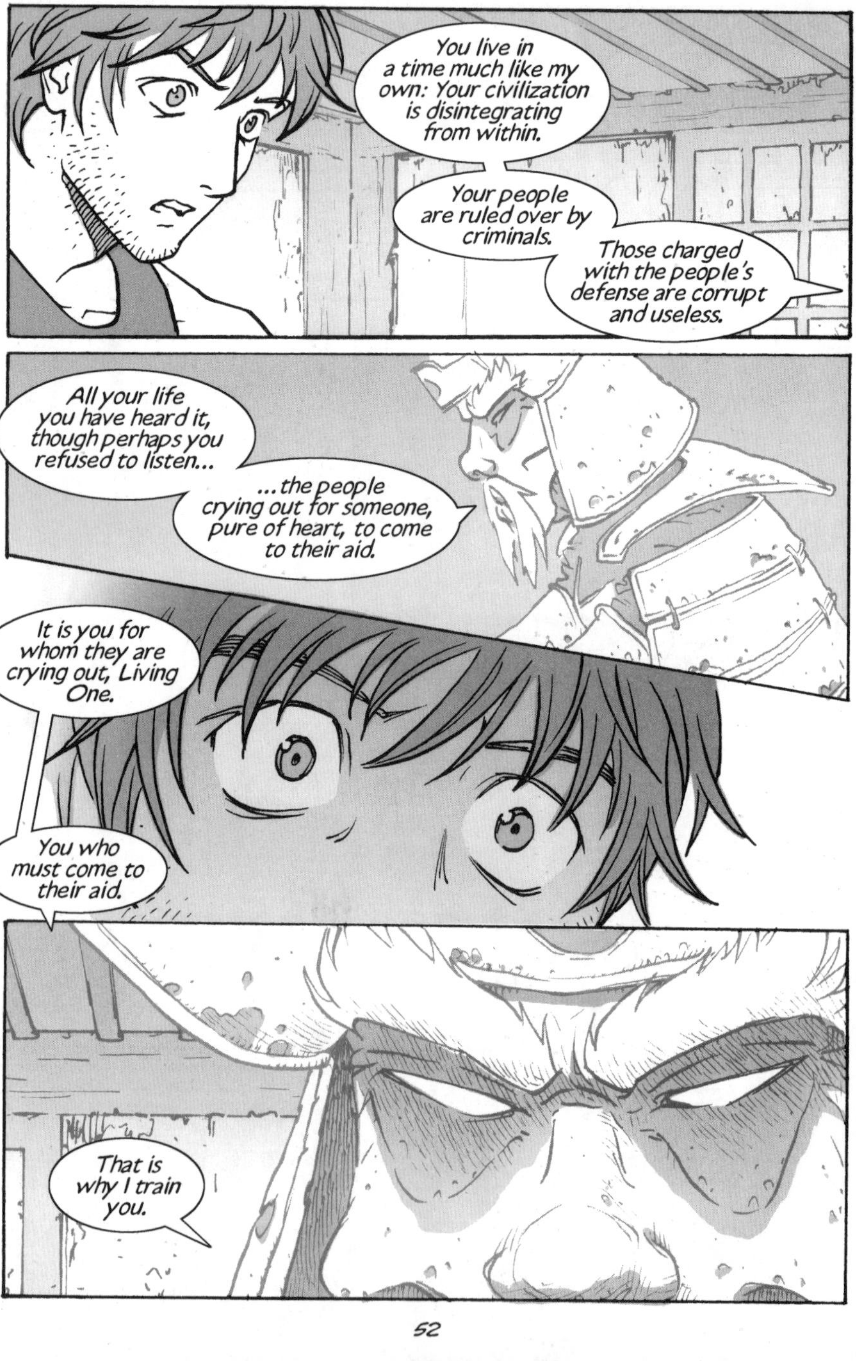
You live in a time much like my own: Your civilization is disintegrating from within.
Your people are ruled over by criminals.
Those charged with the people's defense are corrupt and useless.
All your life you have heard it, though perhaps you refused to listen...
...the people crying out for someone, pure of heart, to come to their aid.
It is you for whom they are crying out, Living One.
You who must come to their aid.
That is why I train you.

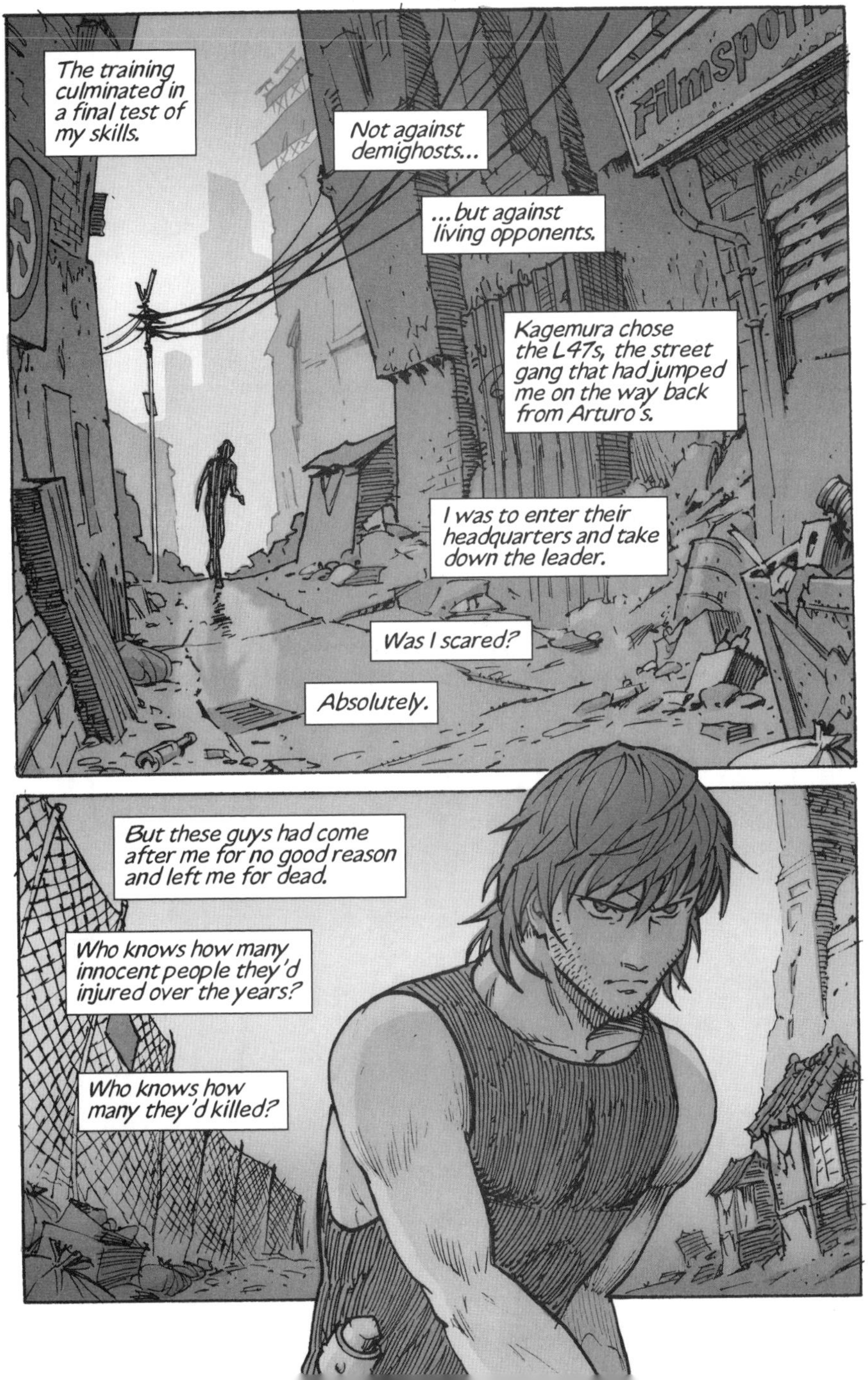

The training culminated in a final test of my skills.
Not against demighosts...
...but against living opponents.
Kagemura chose the L47s, the street gang that had jumped me on the way back from Arturo's.
I was to enter their headquarters and take down the leader.
Was I scared?
Absolutely.
But these guys had come after me for no good reason and left me for dead.
Who knows how many innocent people they'd injured over the years?
Who knows how many they'd killed?

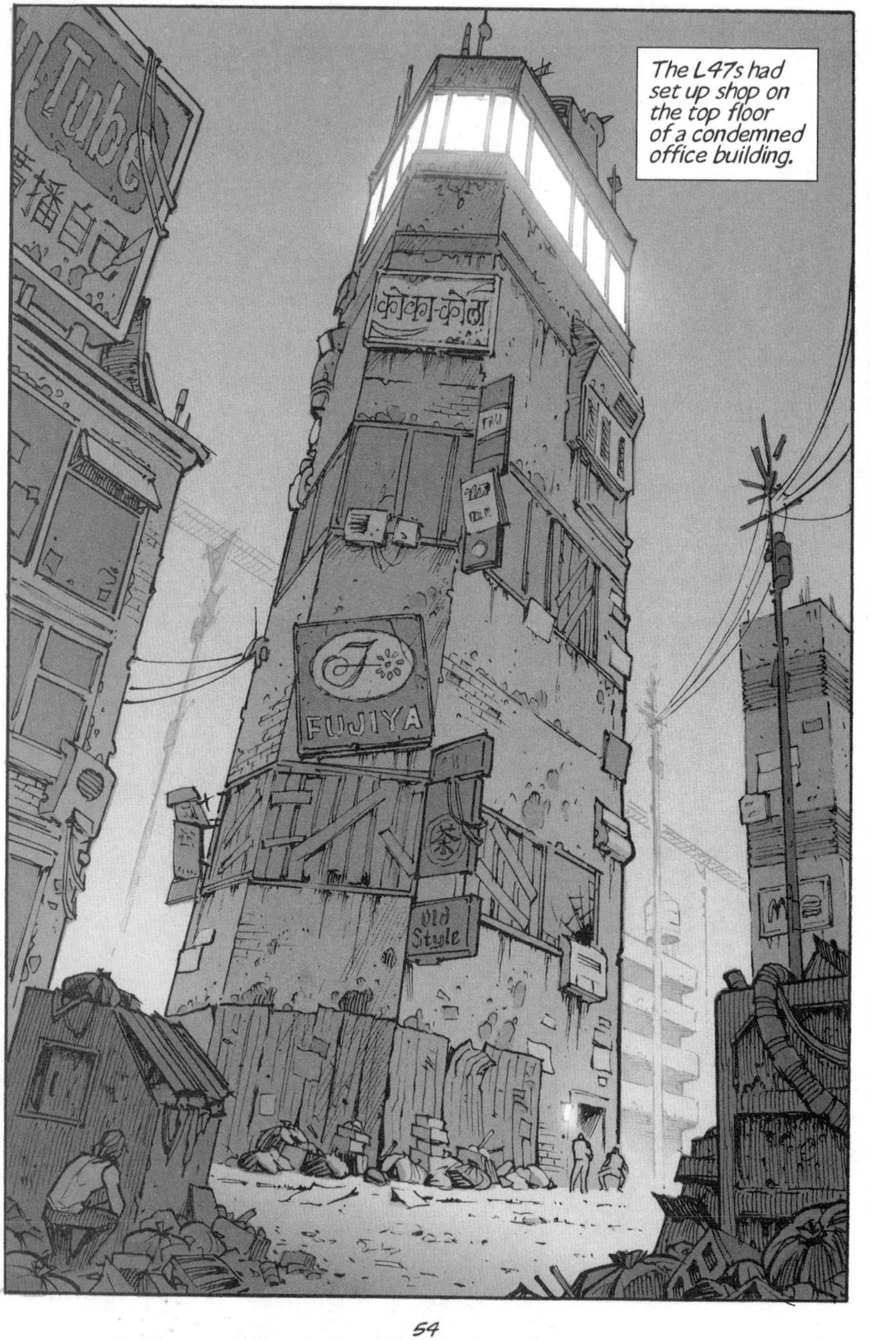
The L47s had set up shop on the top floor of a condemned office building.
कोका-कोला
FUJIYA
Old Style

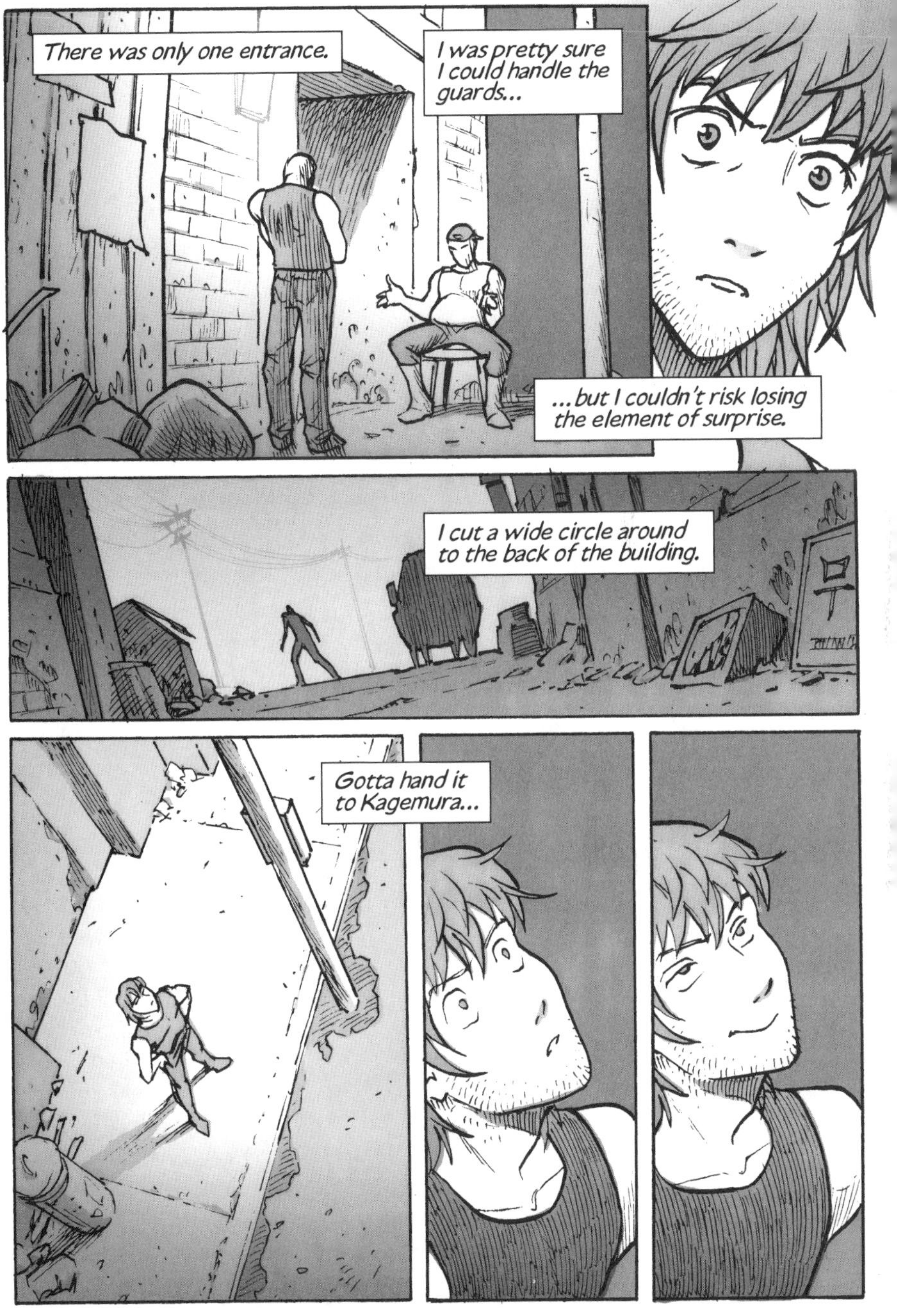
There was only one entrance.
I was pretty sure I could handle the guards...
...but I couldn't risk losing the element of surprise.
I cut a wide circle around to the back of the building.
무
Gotta hand it to Kagemura...

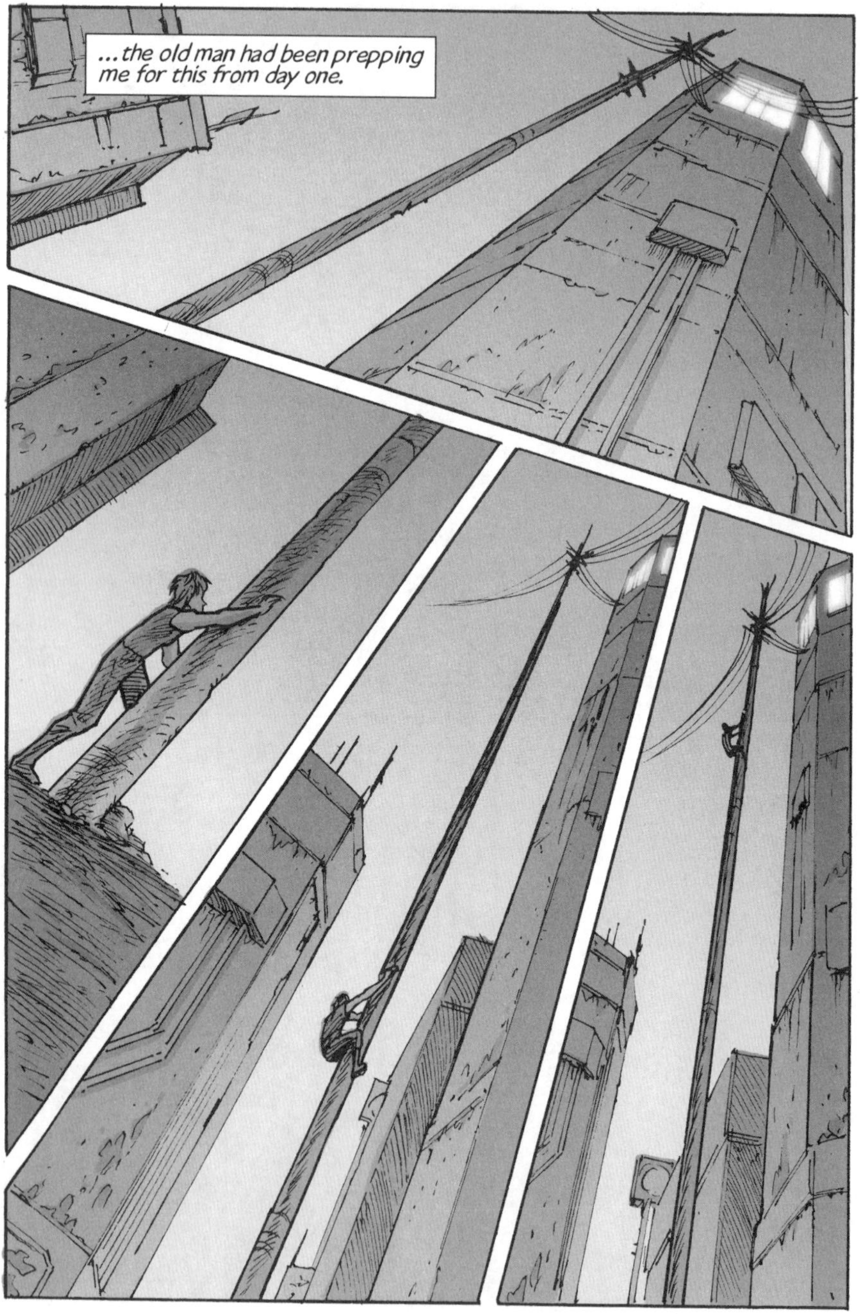
...the old man had been prepping me for this from day one.

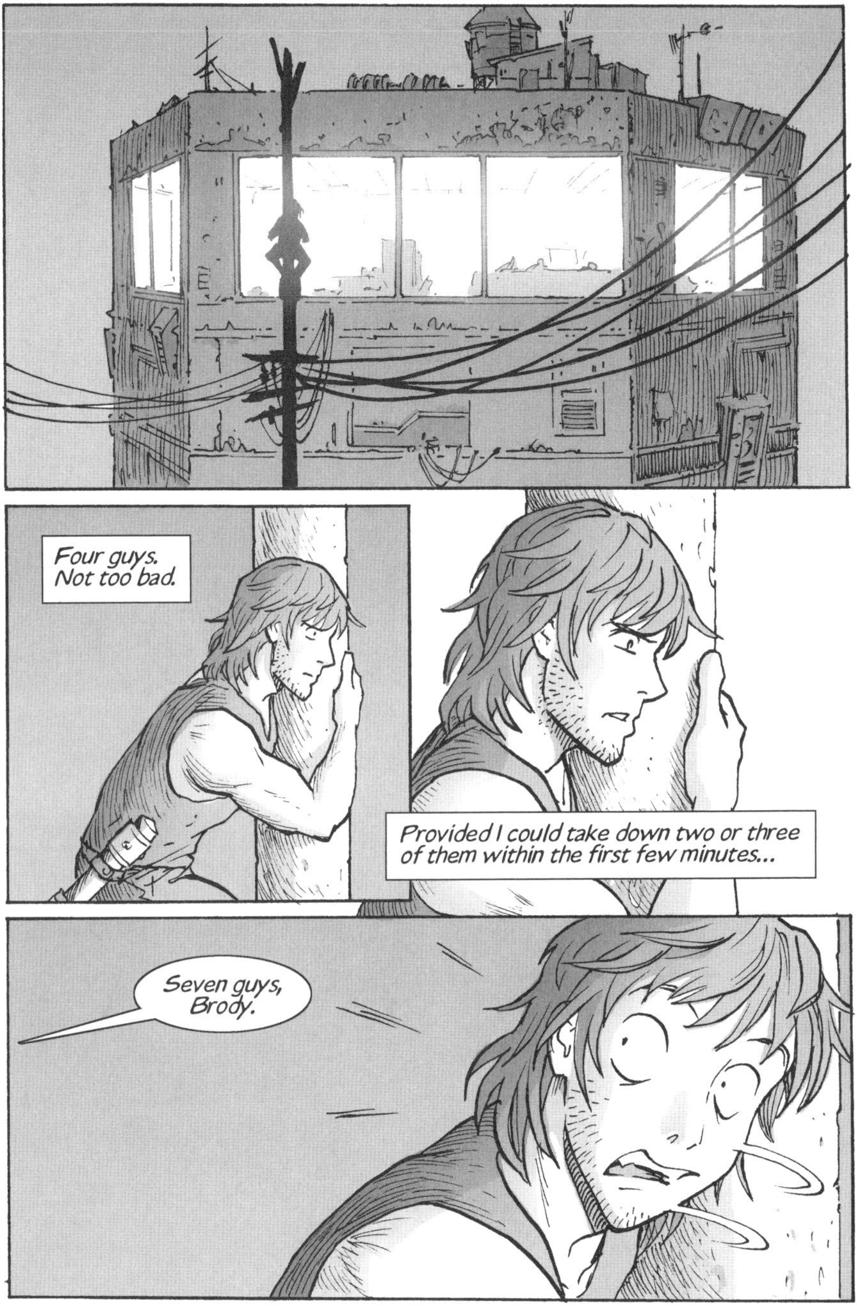
Four guys. Not too bad.
Provided I could take down two or three of them within the first few minutes...
Seven guys, Brody.

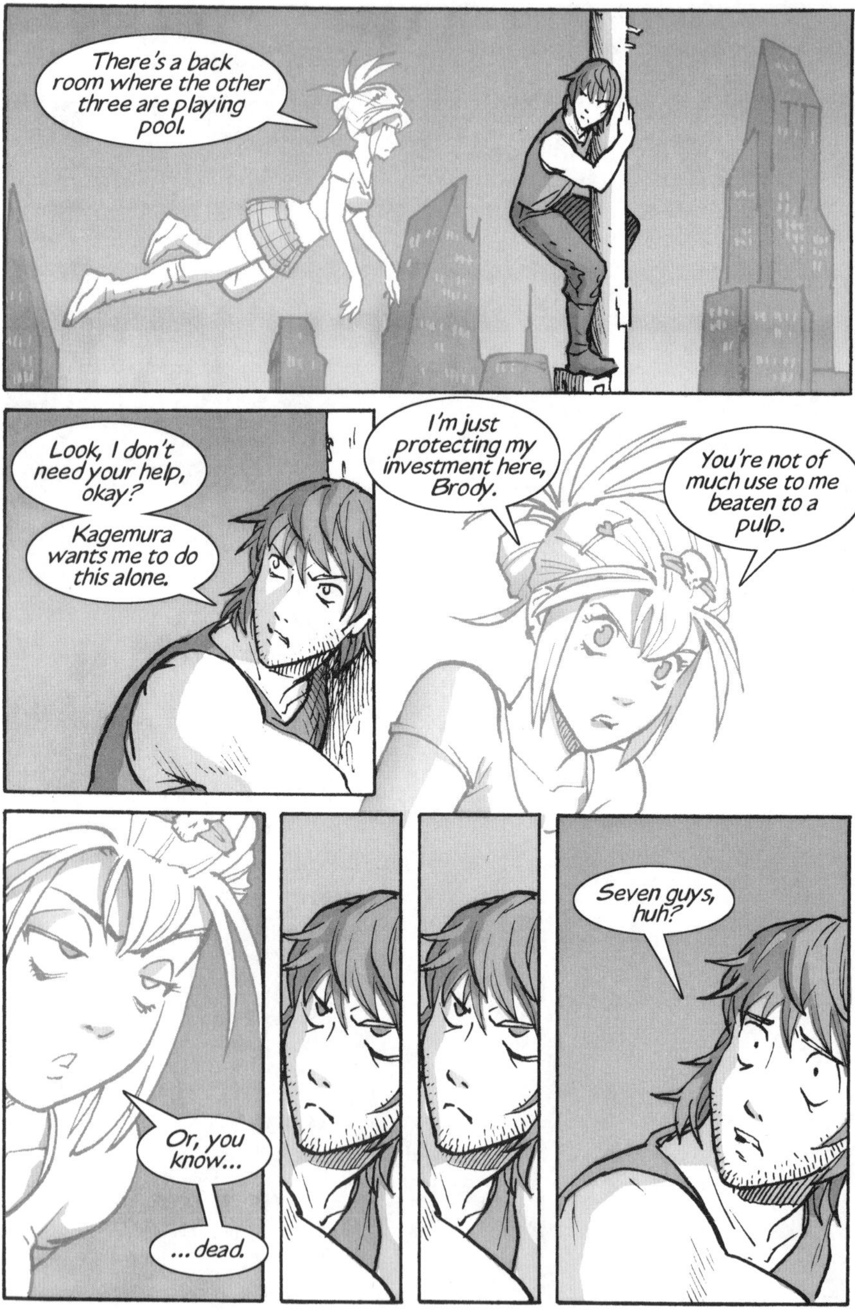
There's a back room where the other three are playing pool.
Look, I don't need your help, okay?
Kagemura wants me to do this alone.
I'm just protecting my investment here, Brody.
You're not of much use to me beaten to a pulp.
Or, you know...
...dead.
Seven guys, huh?

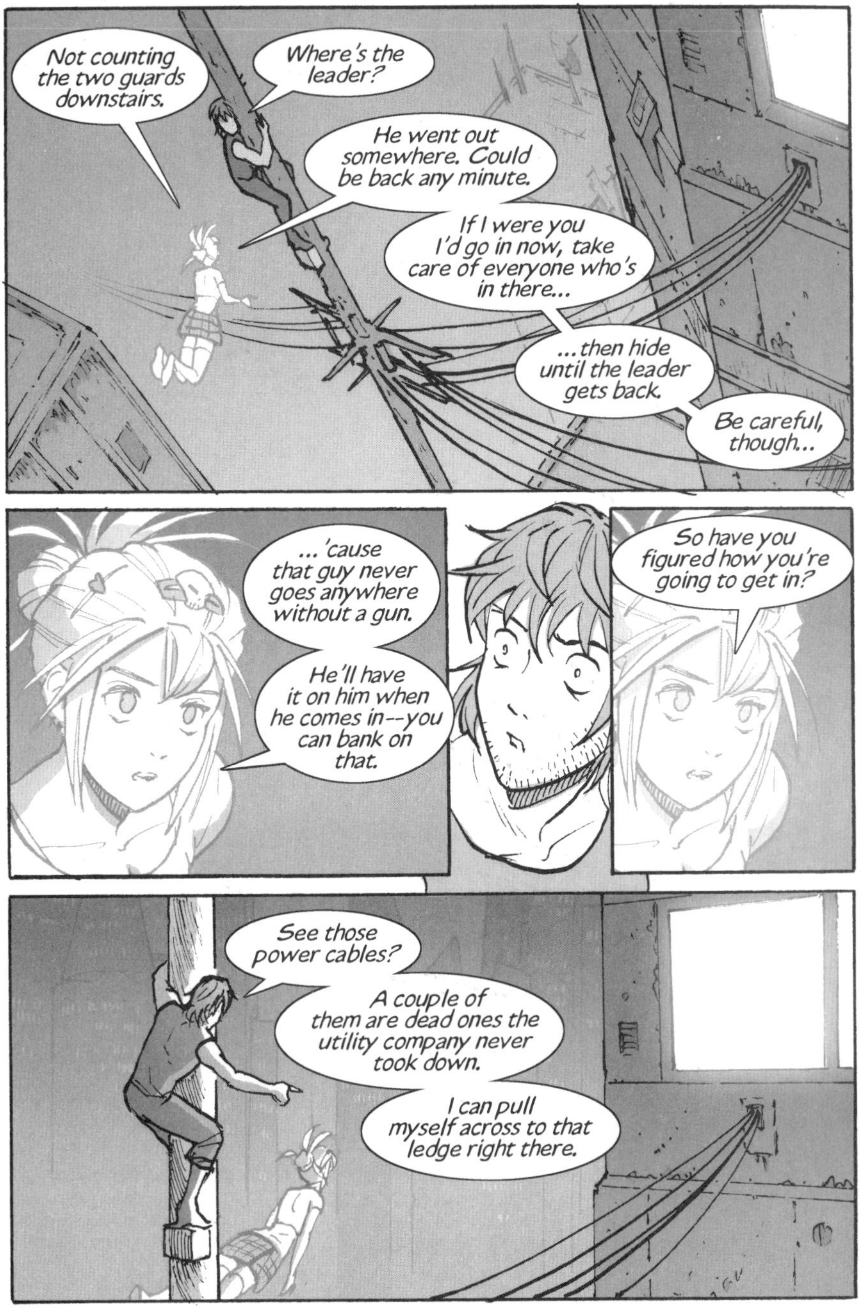
Not counting the two guards downstairs.
Where's the leader?
He went out somewhere. Could be back any minute.
If I were you I'd go in now, take care of everyone who's in there...
...then hide until the leader gets back.
Be careful, though...
...'cause that guy never goes anywhere without a gun.
He'll have it on him when he comes in--you can bank on that.
So have you figured how you're going to get in?
See those power cables?
A couple of them are dead ones the utility company never took down.
I can pull myself across to that ledge right there.

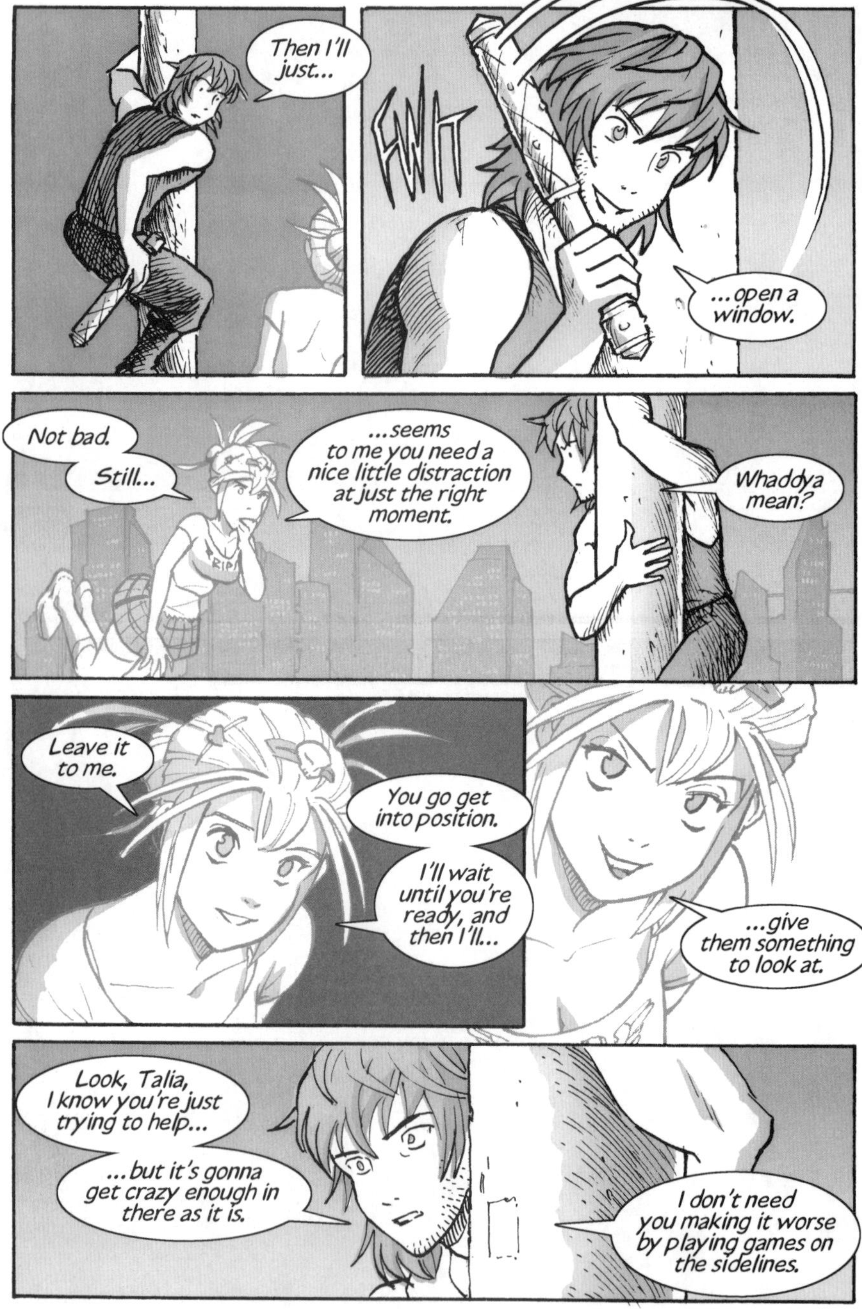
Then I'll just...
FWIT
...open a window.
Not bad.
Still...
...seems to me you need a nice little distraction at just the right moment.
Whaddya mean?
Leave it to me.
You go get into position.
I'll wait until you're ready, and then I'll...
...give them something to look at.
Look, Talia, I know you're just trying to help...
...but it's gonna get crazy enough in there as it is.
I don't need you making it worse by playing games on the sidelines.

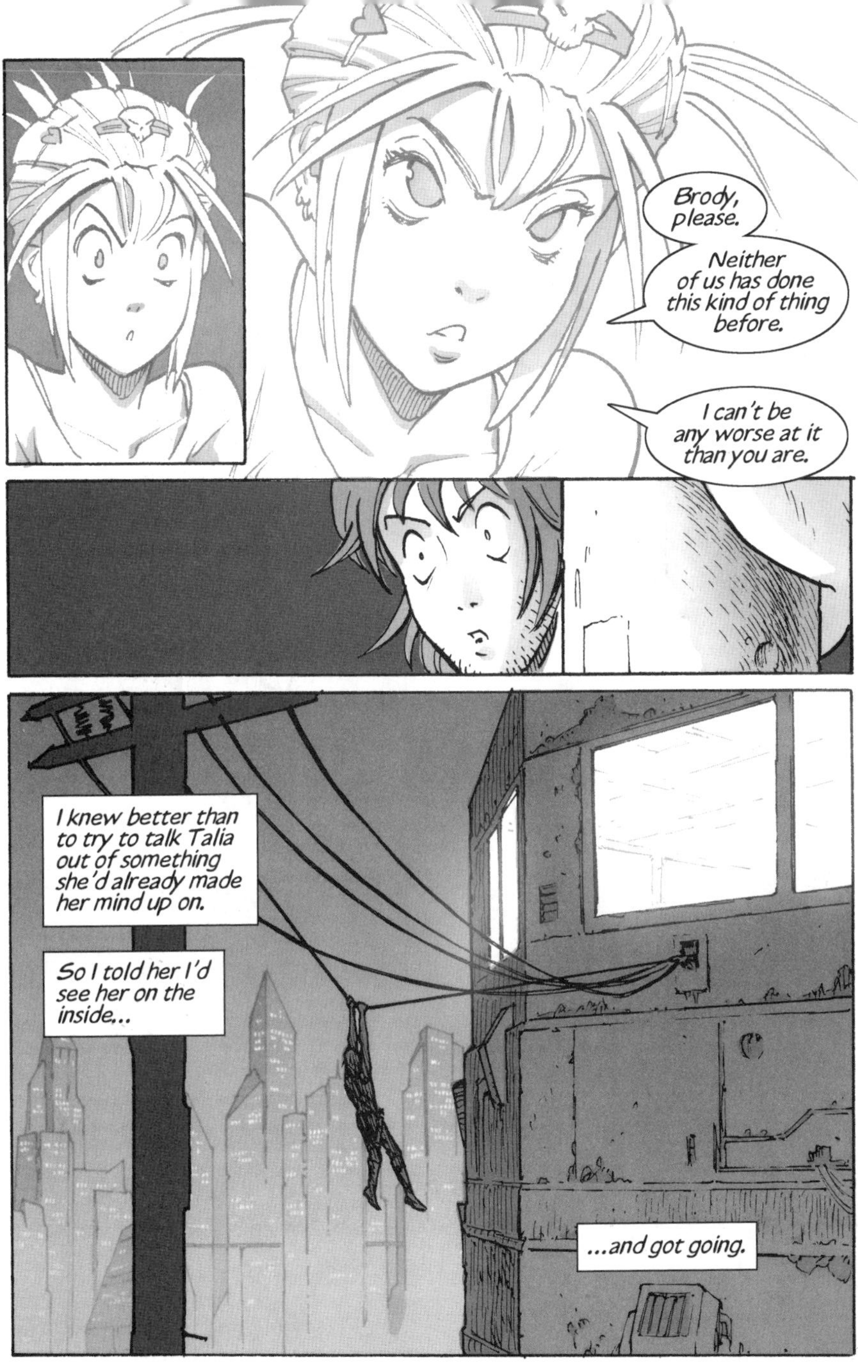

Brody, please.
Neither of us has done this kind of thing before.
I can't be any worse at it than you are.
I knew better than to try to talk Talia out of something she'd already made her mind up on.
So I told her I'd see her on the inside...
...and got going.

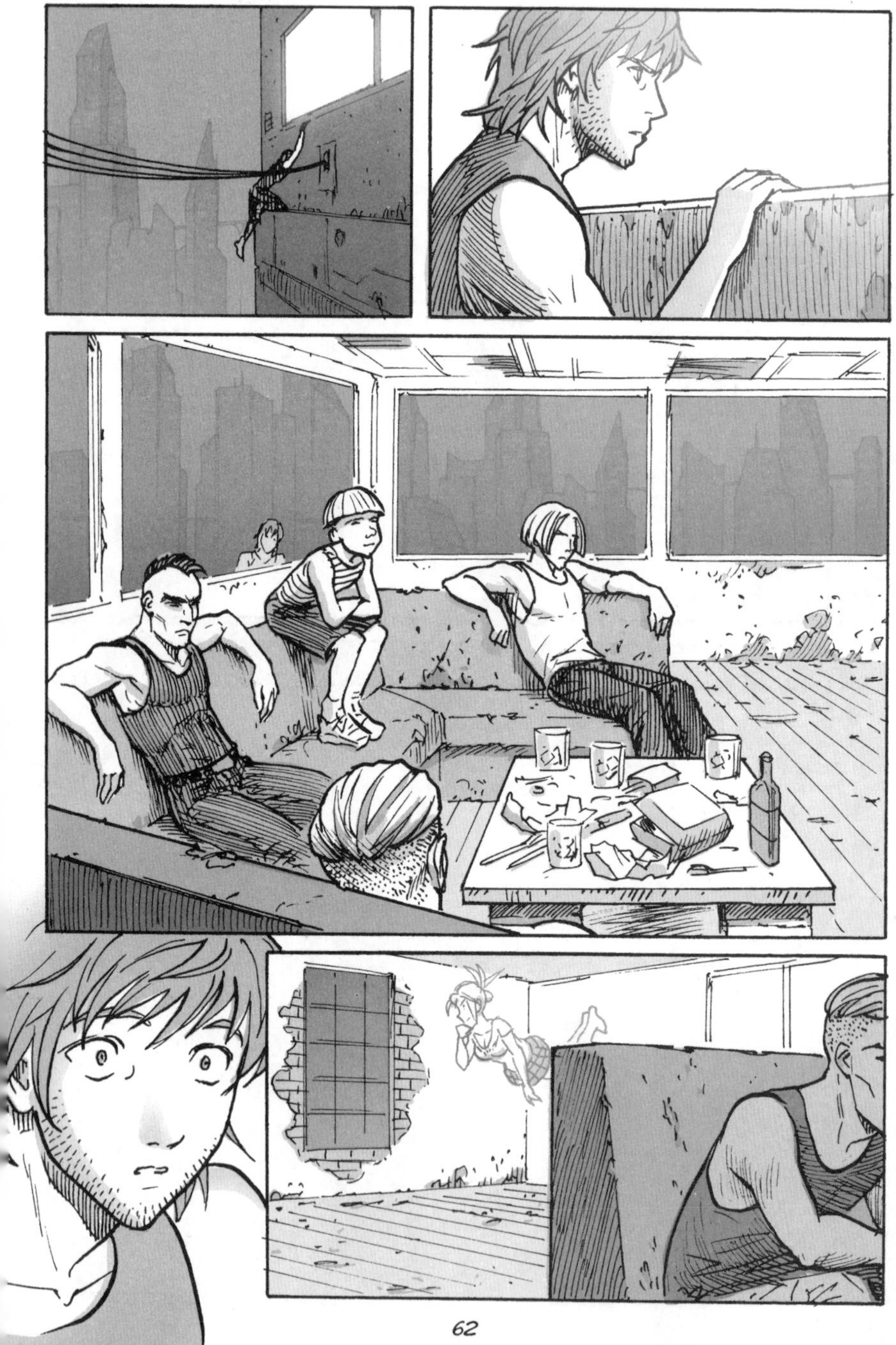

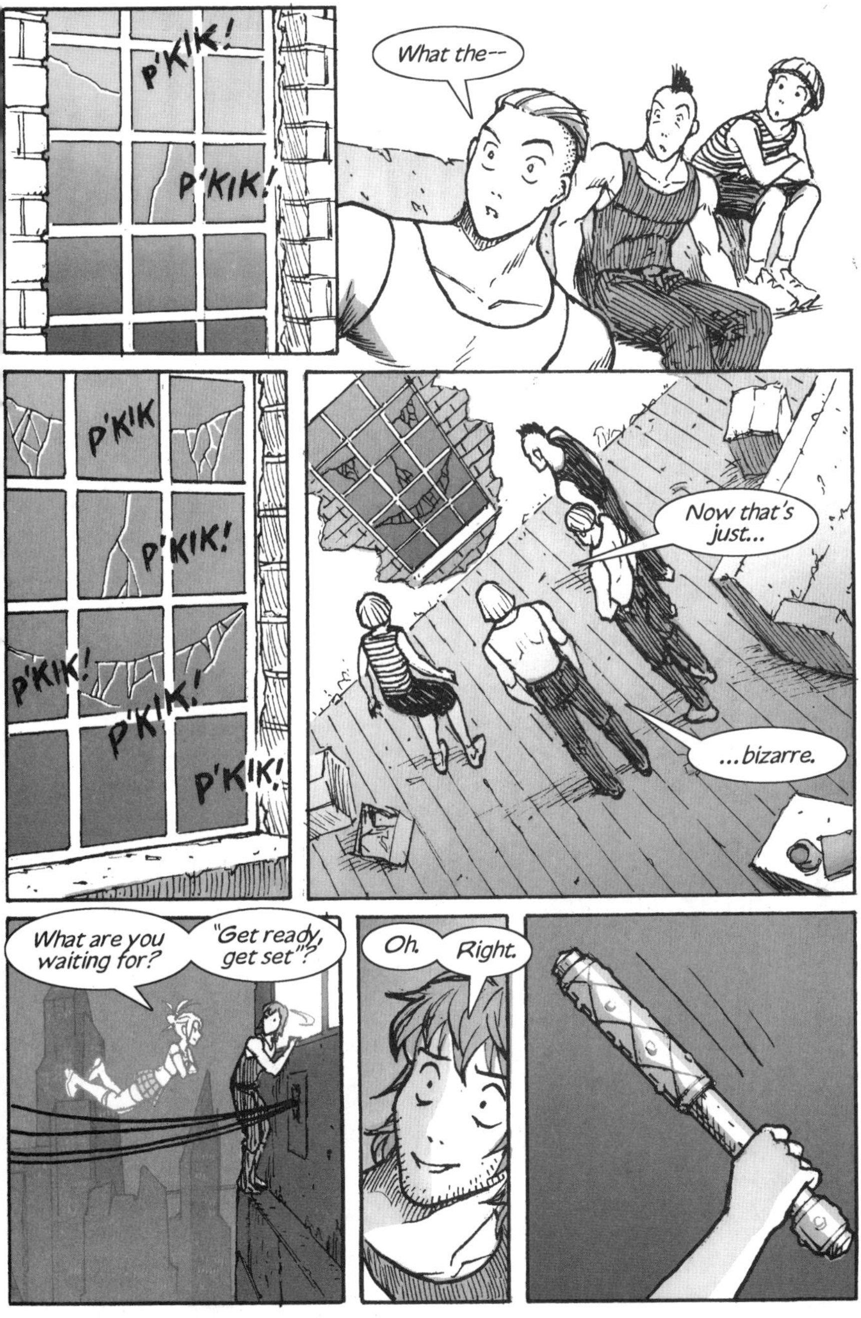
P'KIK!
P'KIK!
What the--
P'KIK
P'KIK!
P'KIK!
P'KIK!
P'KIK!
Now that's just...
...bizarre.
What are you waiting for?
"Get ready, get set"?
Oh.
Right.

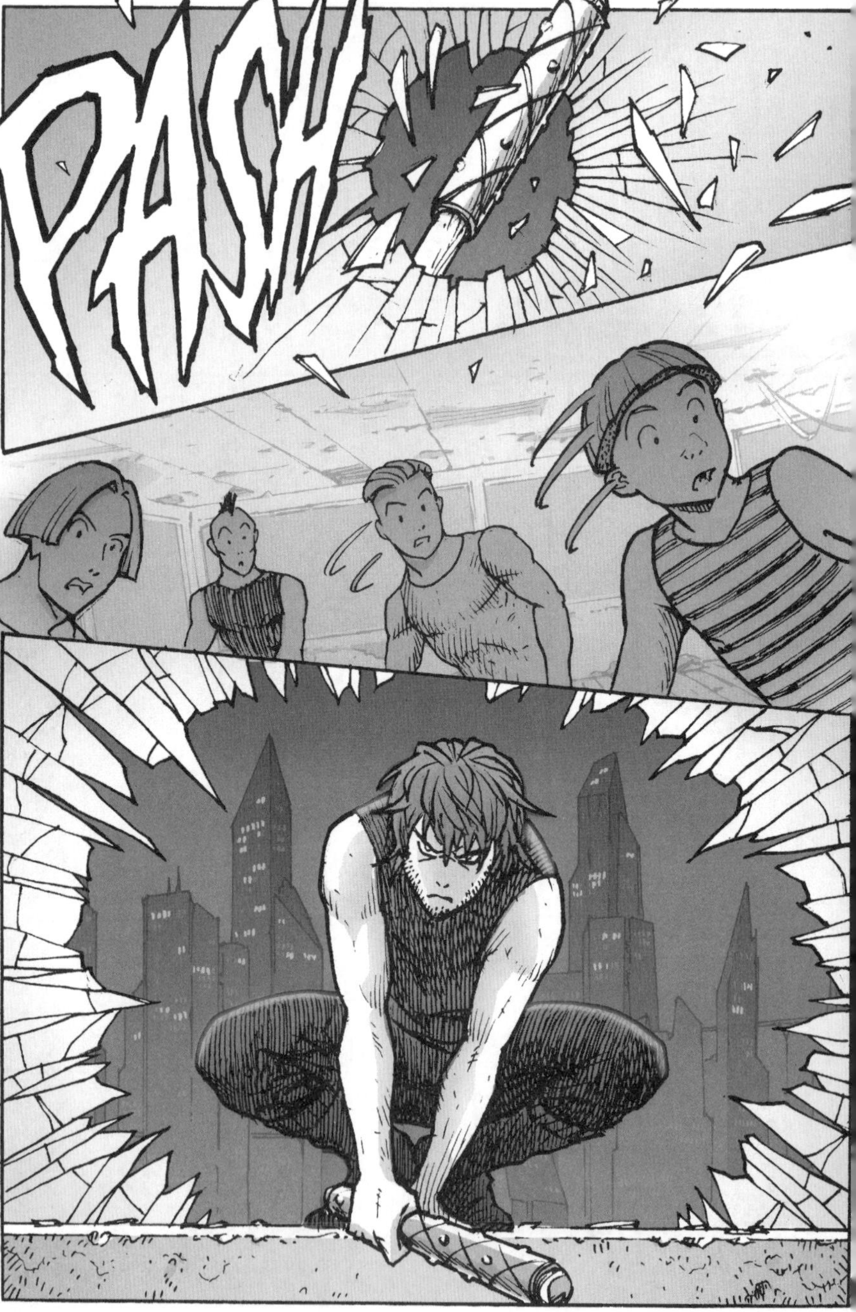
PASH

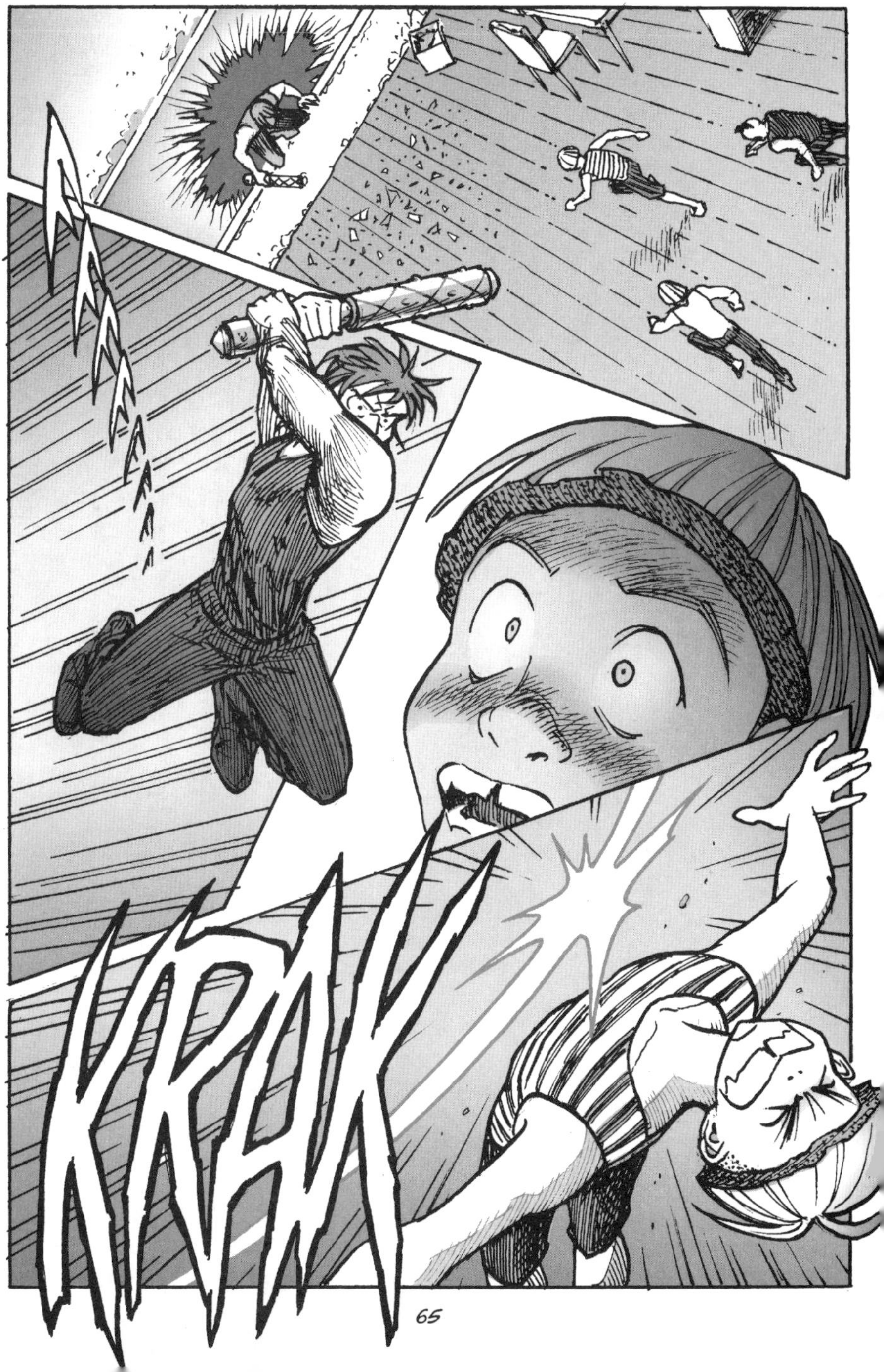
KRAK

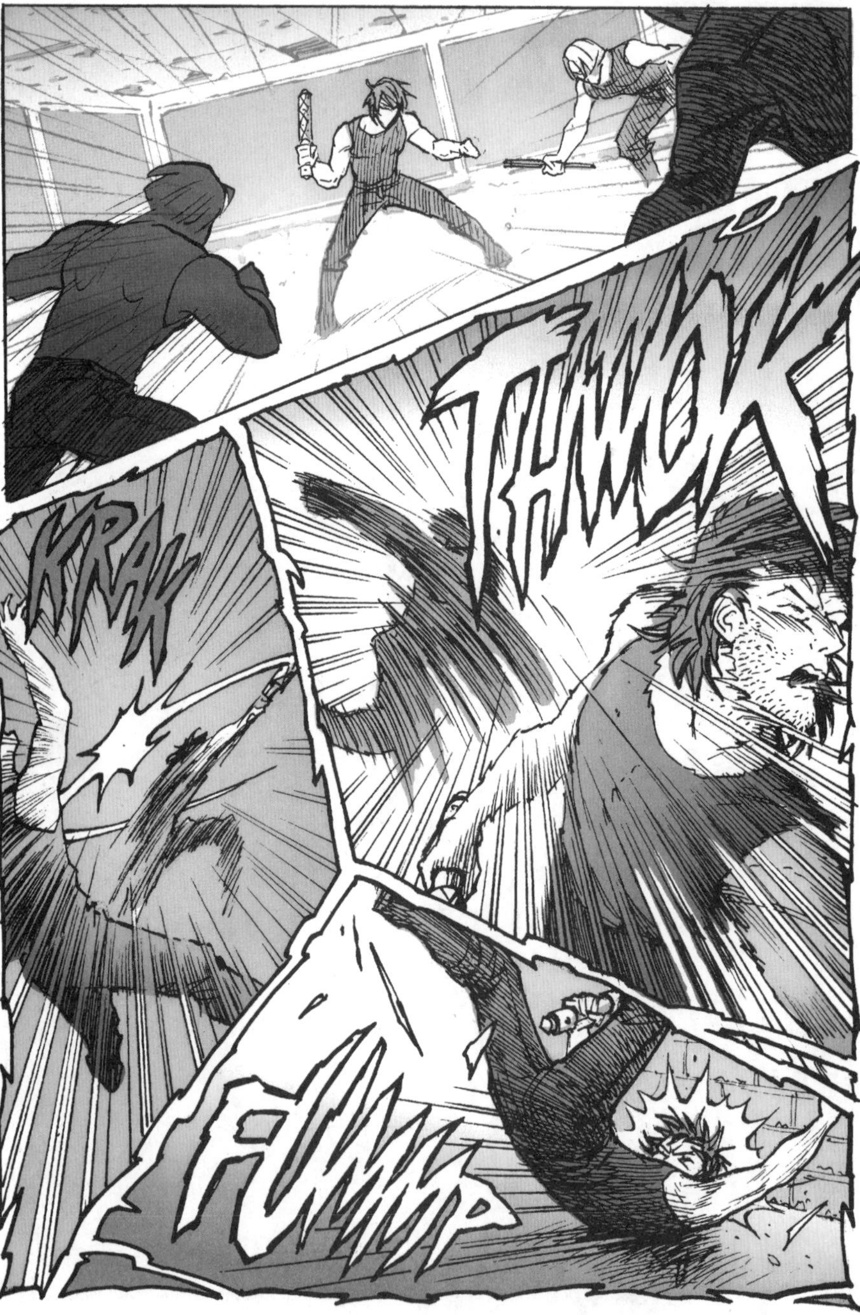
THUNK
KRAK
FUMMP

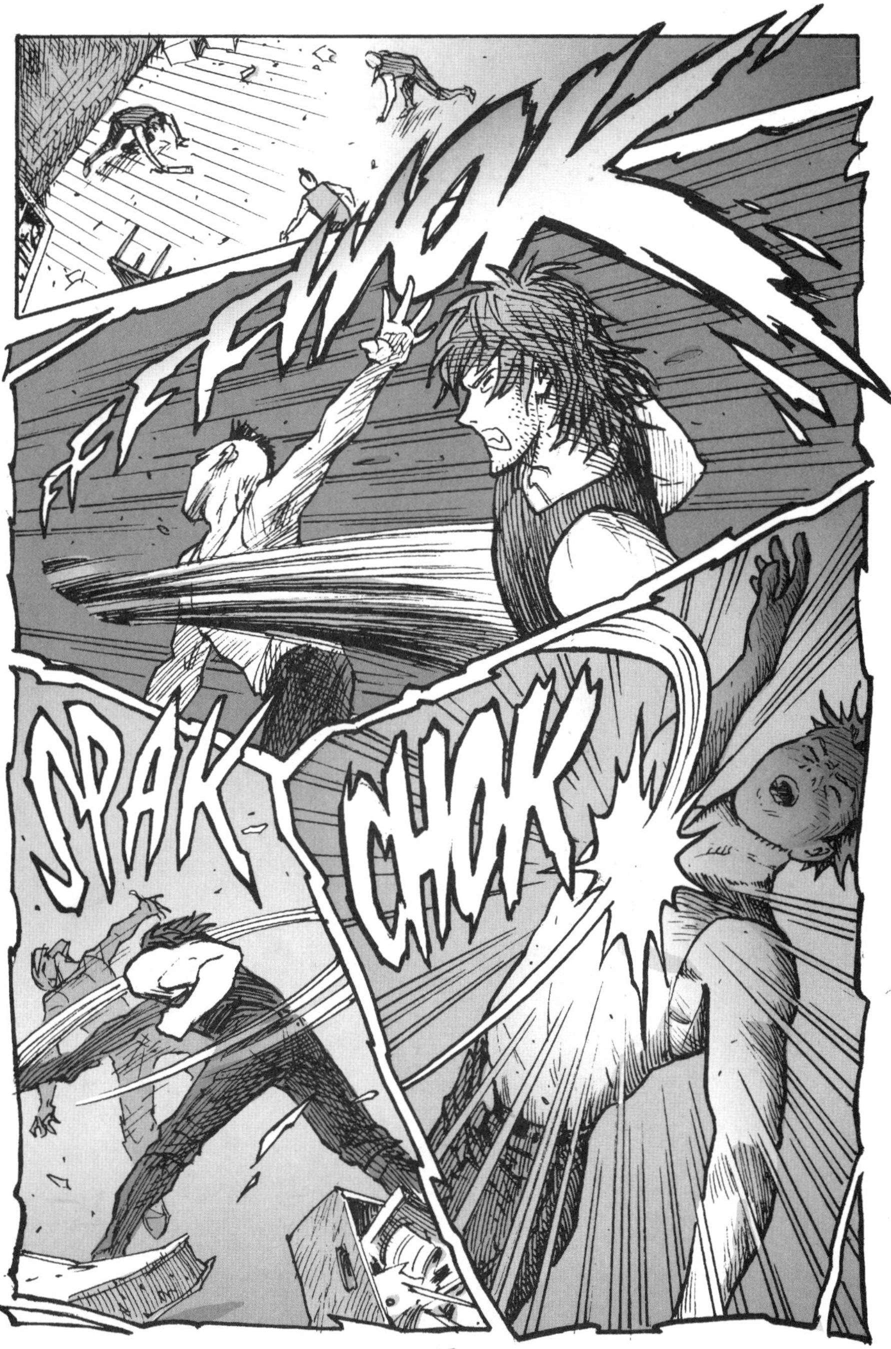
FFFWOK
SPAK
CHOK

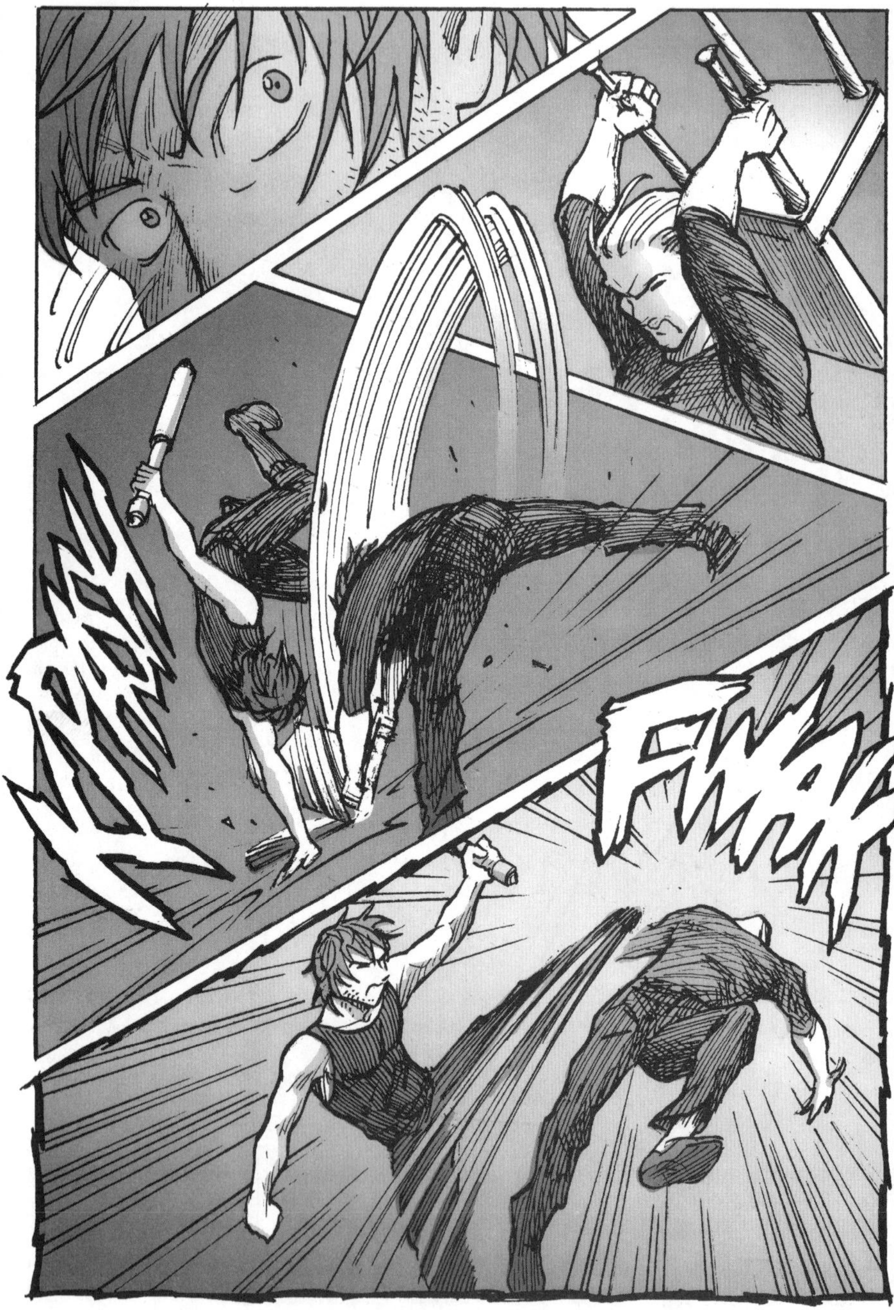
FWAK

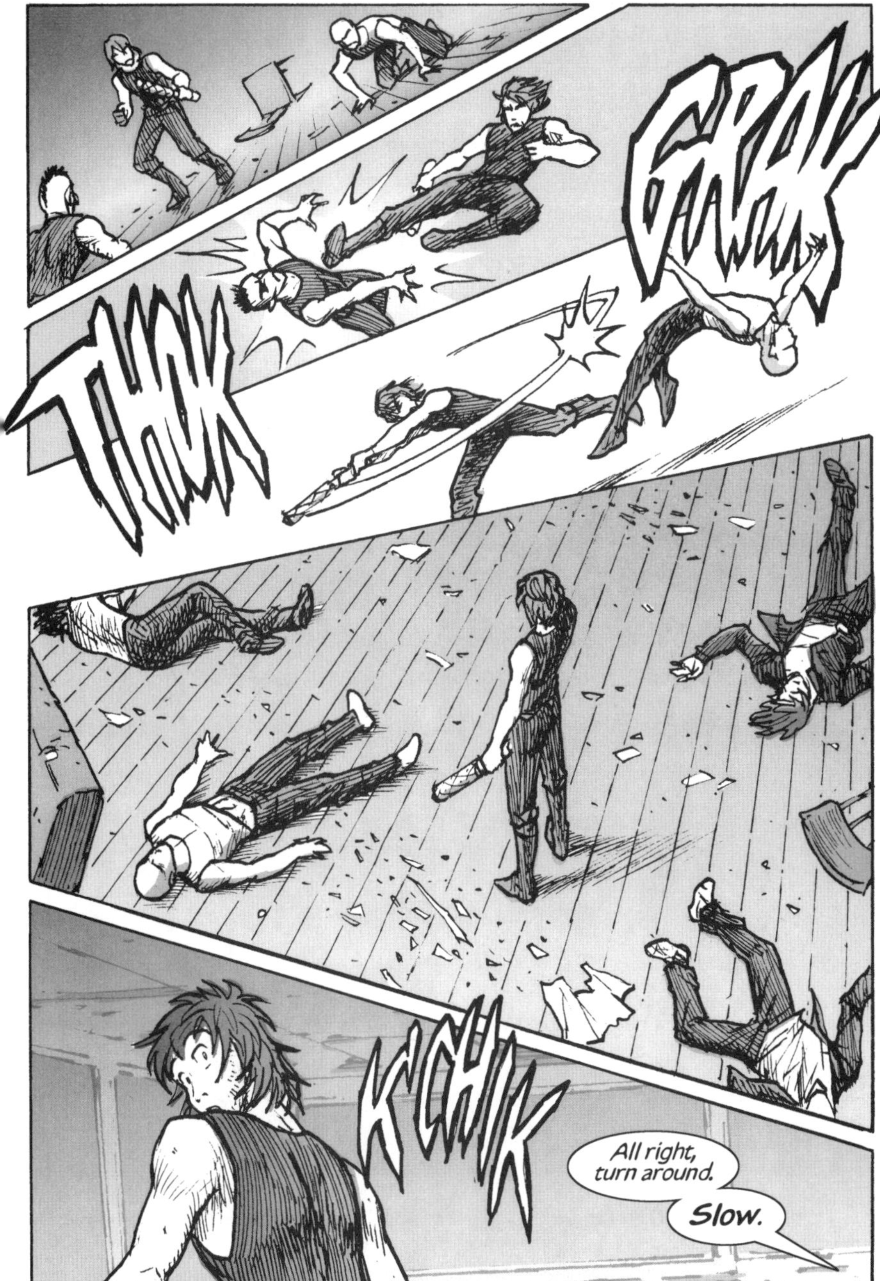
CRAAAK
THUK
K'CHIK
All right, turn around.
Slow.

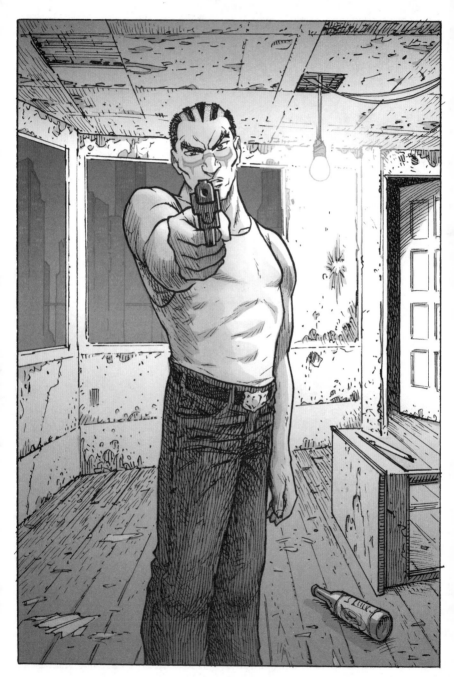

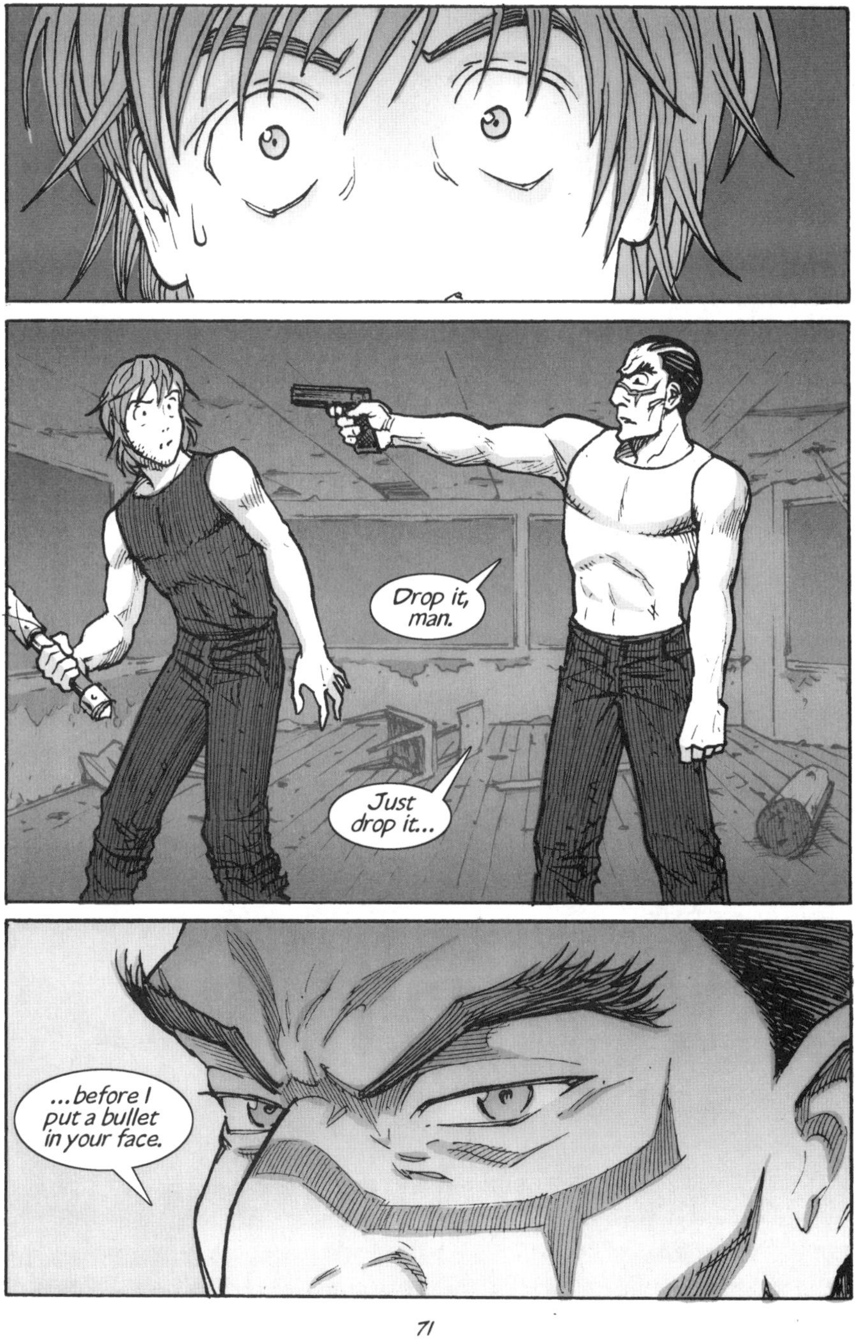
Drop it, man.
Just drop it...
...before I put a bullet in your face.

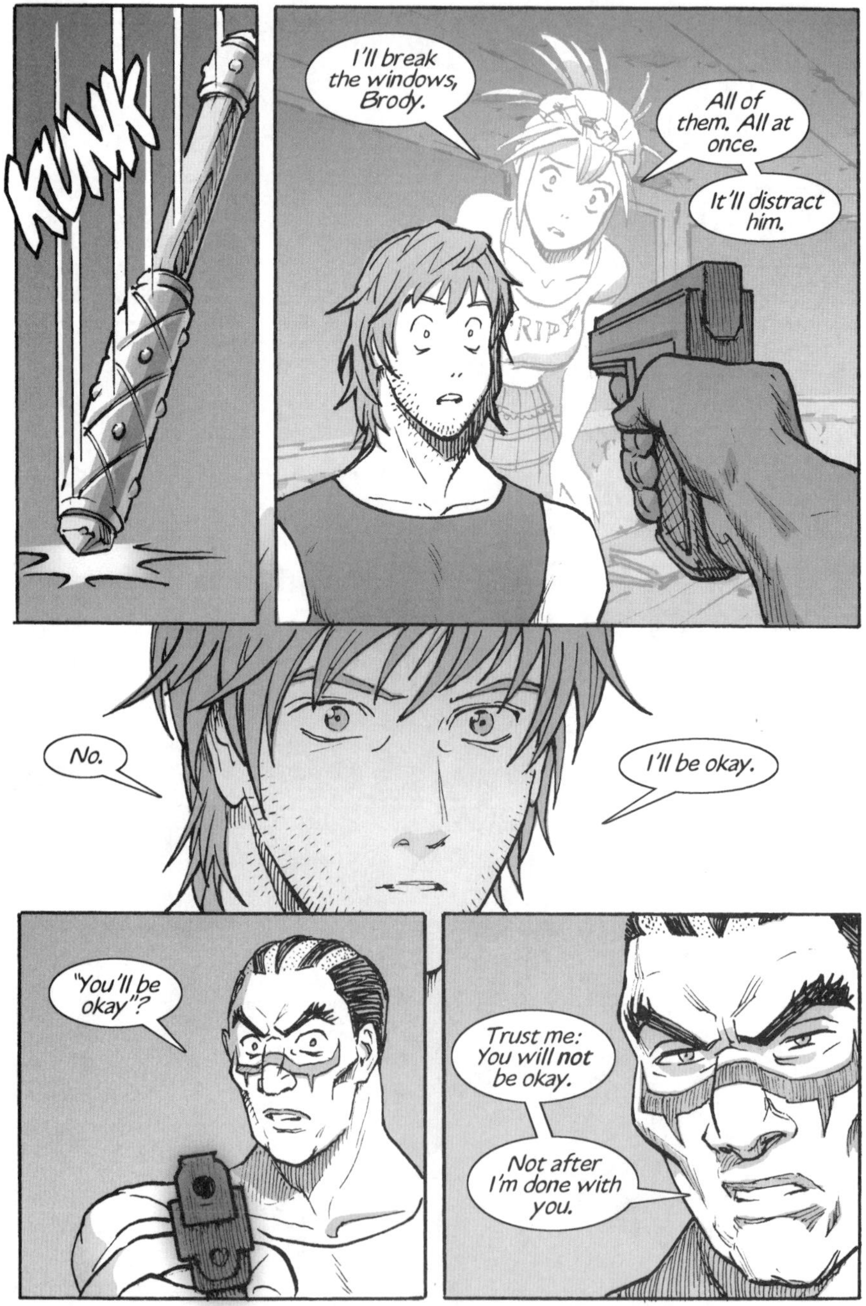
KLUNK
I'll break the windows, Brody.
All of them. All at once.
It'll distract him.
RIP
No.
I'll be okay.
"You'll be okay"?
Trust me: You will **not** be okay.
Not after I'm done with you.

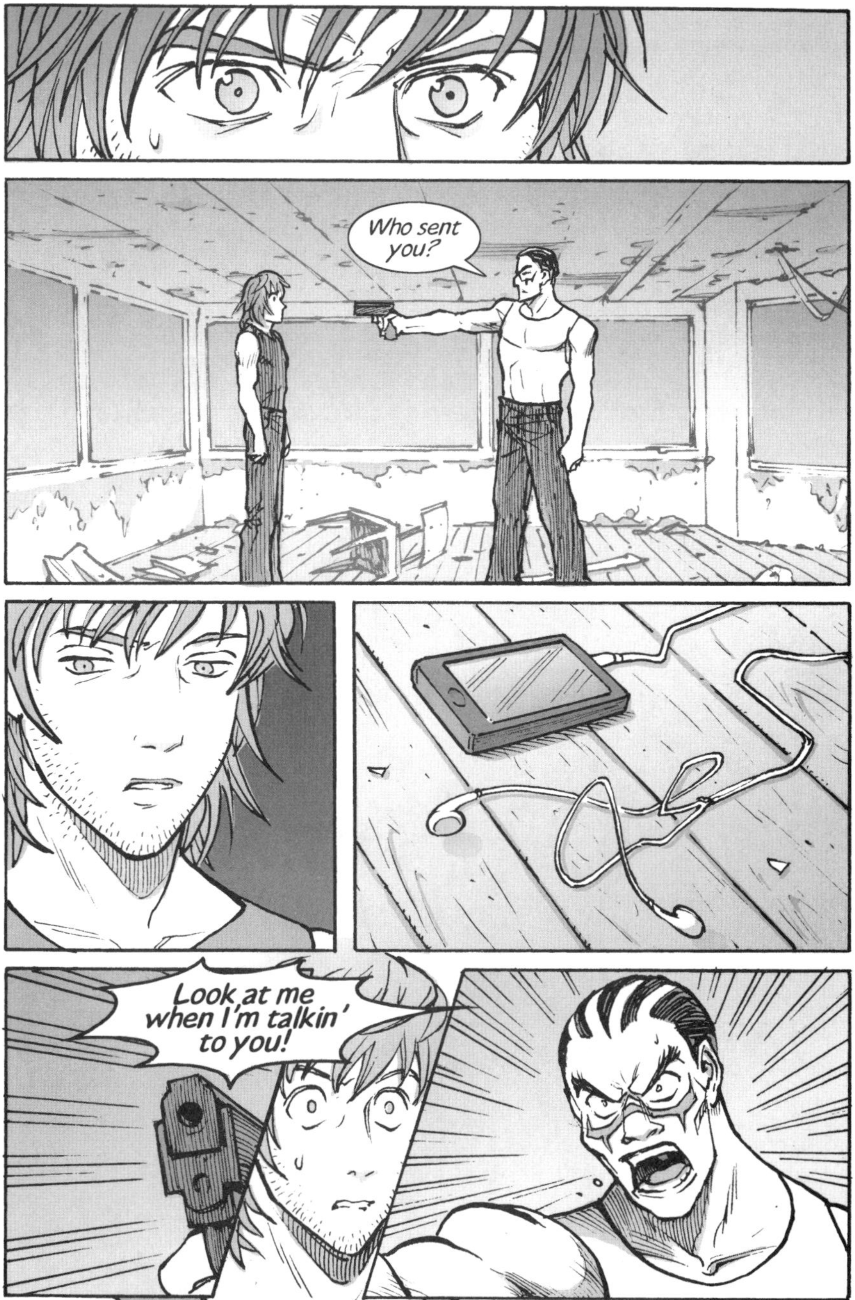
Who sent you?
Look at me when I'm talkin' to you!

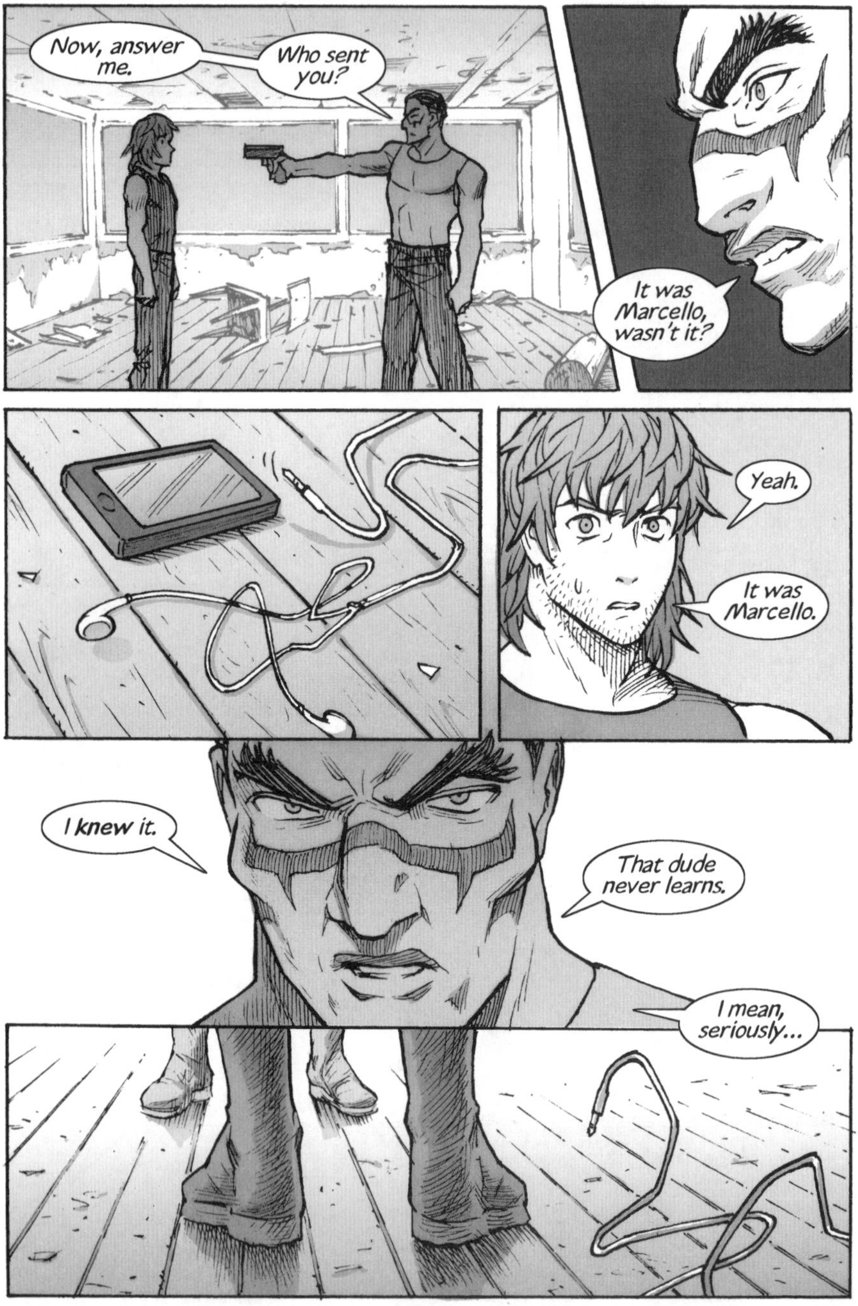
Now, answer me.
Who sent you?
It was Marcello, wasn't it?
Yeah.
It was Marcello.
I **knew** it.
That dude never learns.
I mean, seriously...

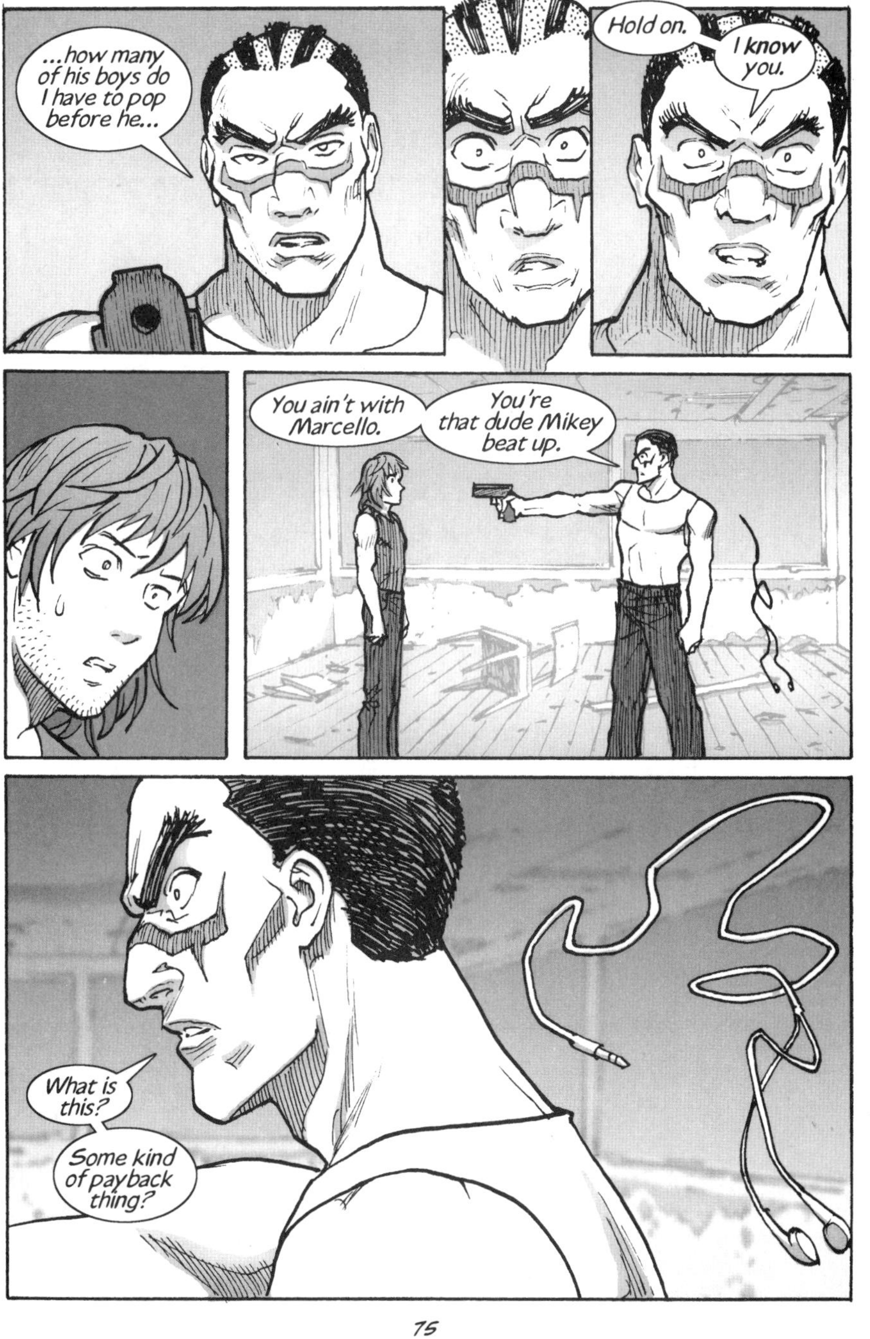
...how many of his boys do I have to pop before he...
Hold on.
I know you.
You ain't with Marcello.
You're that dude Mikey beat up.
What is this?
Some kind of payback thing?

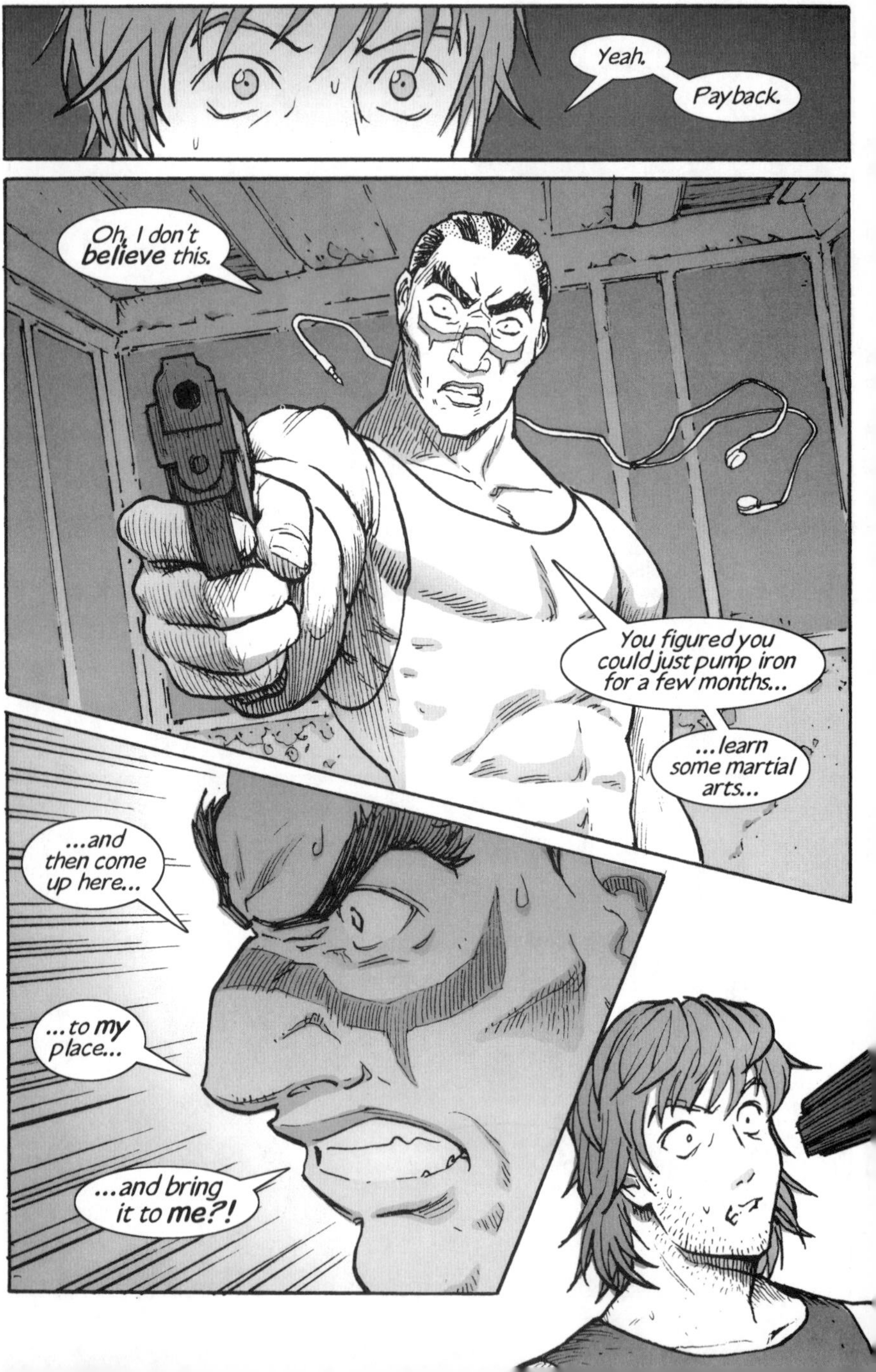
Yeah.
Payback.
Oh, I don't **believe** this.
You figured you could just pump iron for a few months...
...learn some martial arts...
...and then come up here...
...to **my** place...
...and bring it to **me?!**

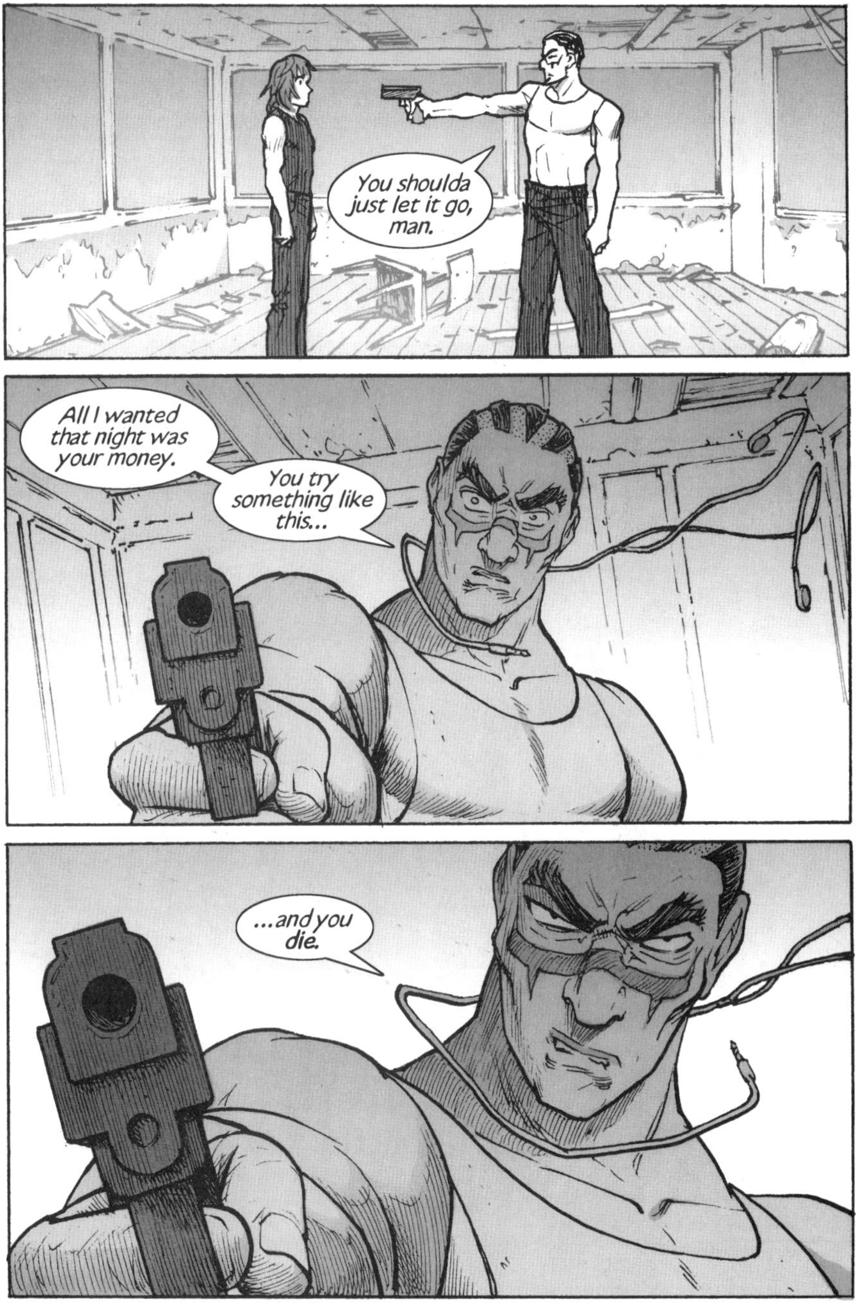
You shoulda just let it go, man.
All I wanted that night was your money.
You try something like this...
...and you die.

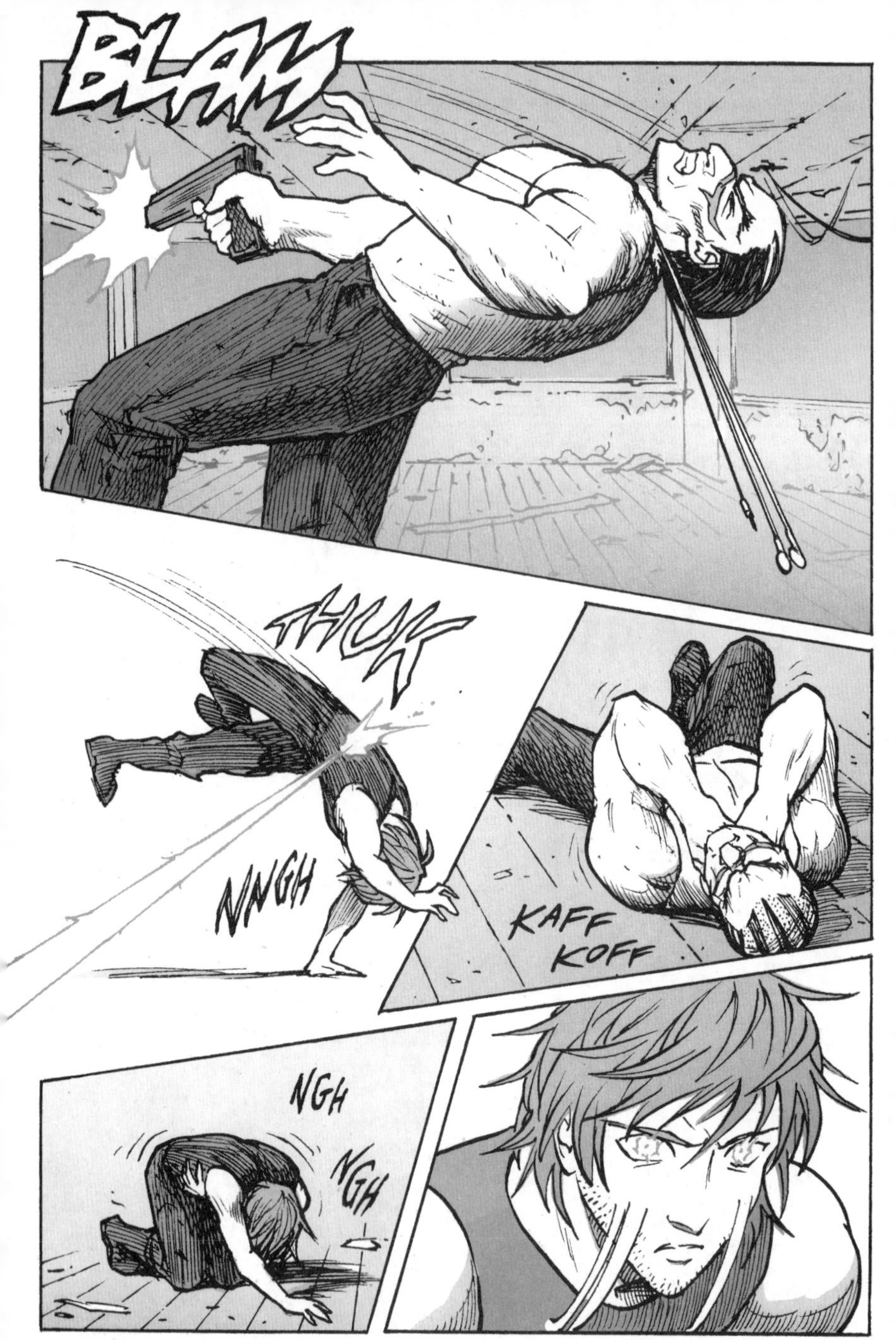
BLAM
THUK
NNGH
KAFF
KOFF
NGH
NGH

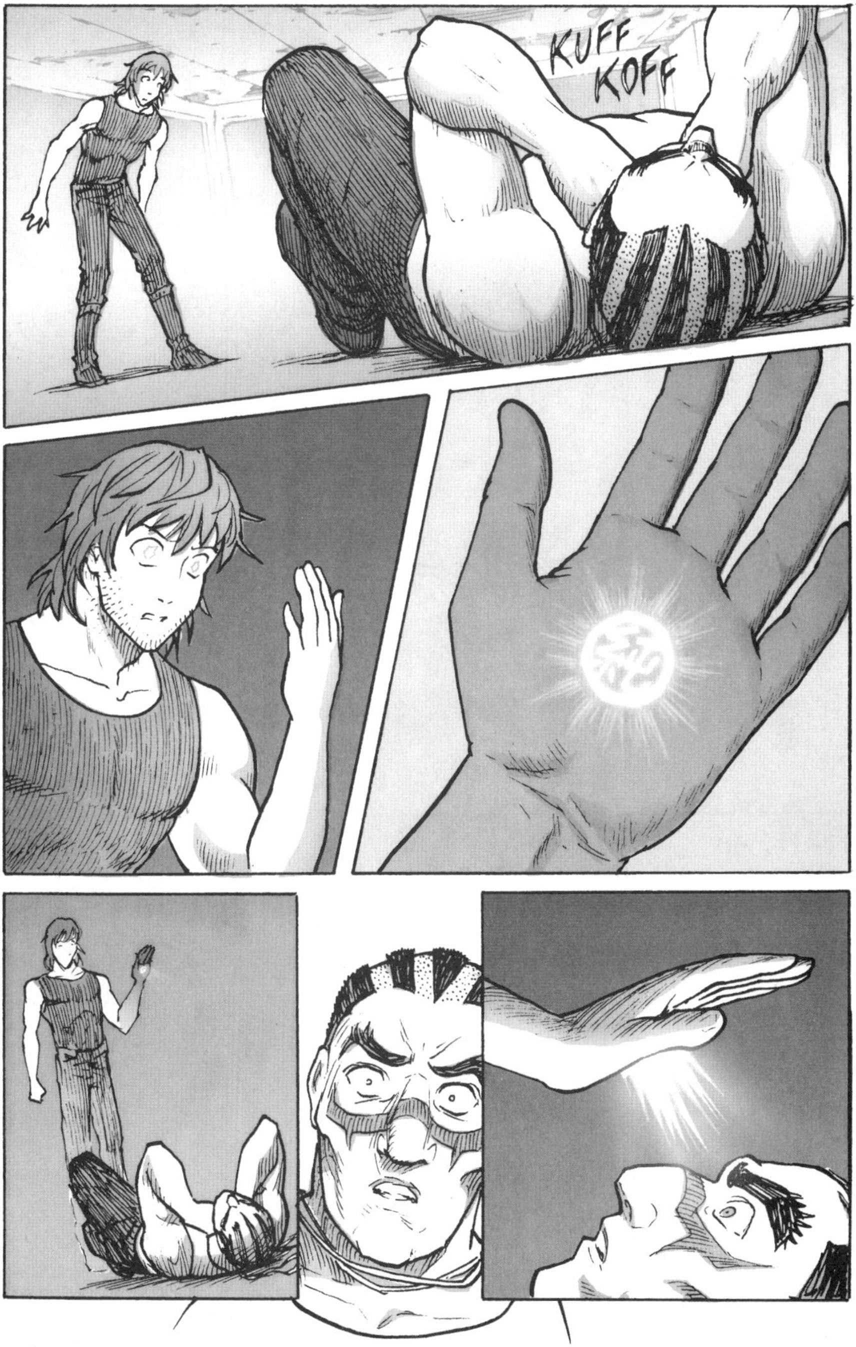
KUFF
KOFF

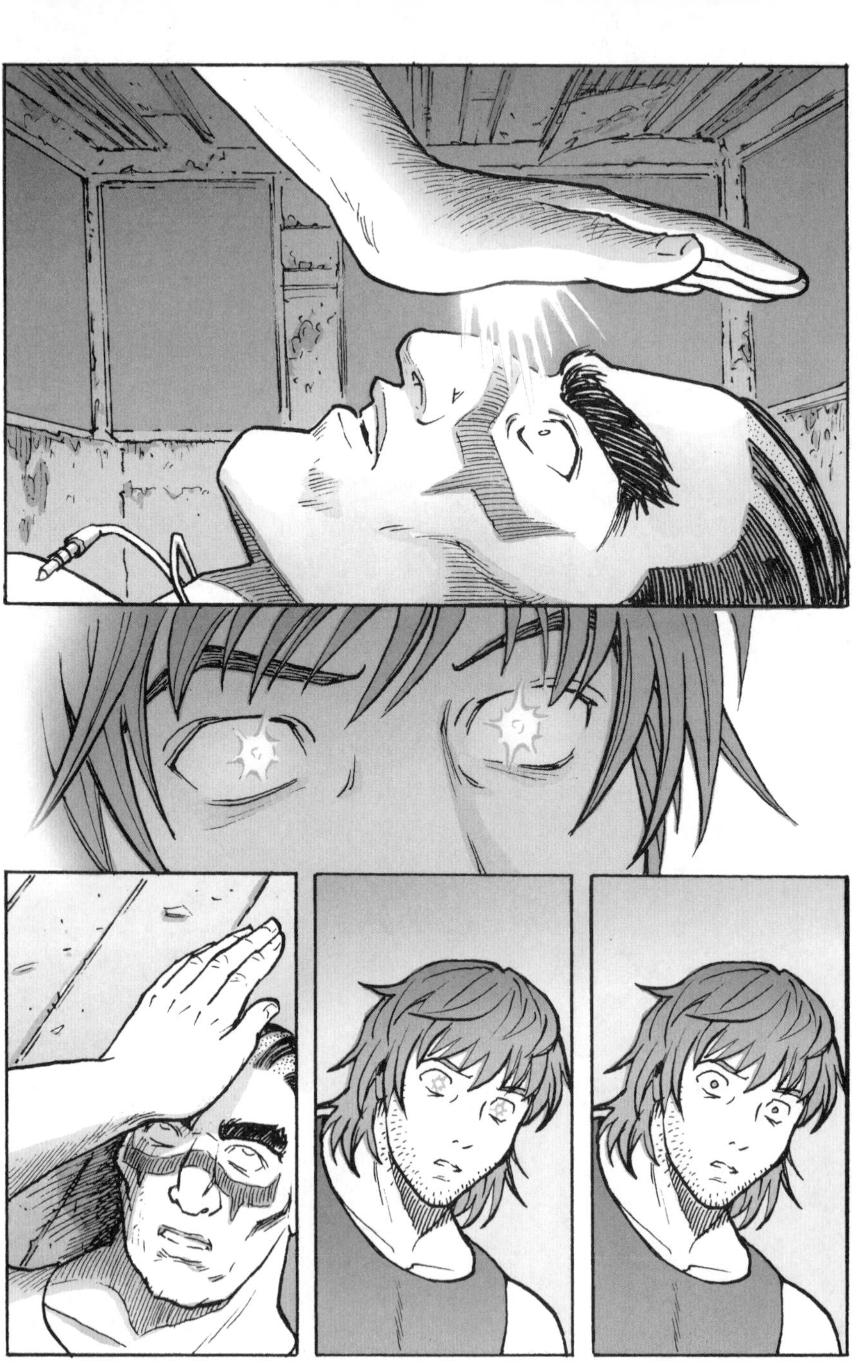

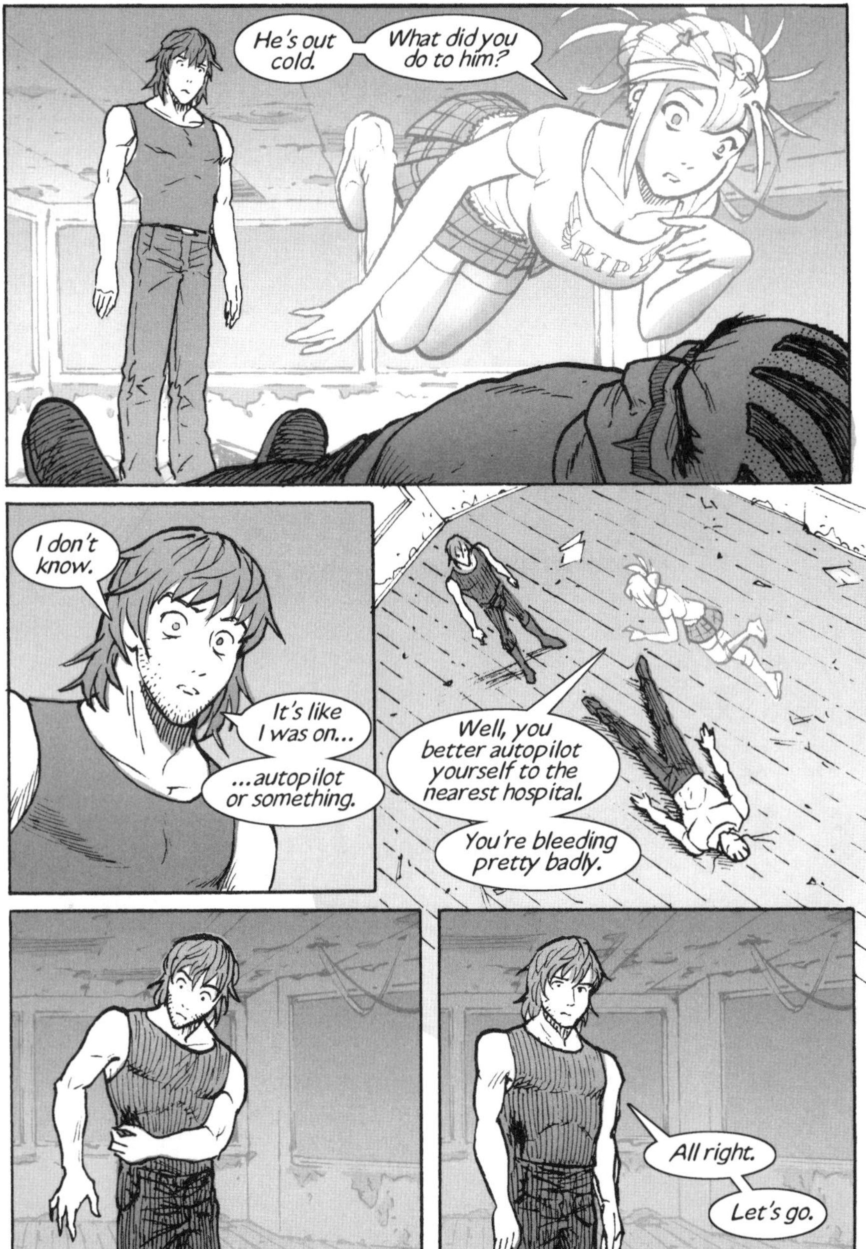
He's out cold.
What did you do to him?
I don't know.
It's like I was on...
...autopilot or something.
Well, you better autopilot yourself to the nearest hospital.
You're bleeding pretty badly.
All right.
Let's go.

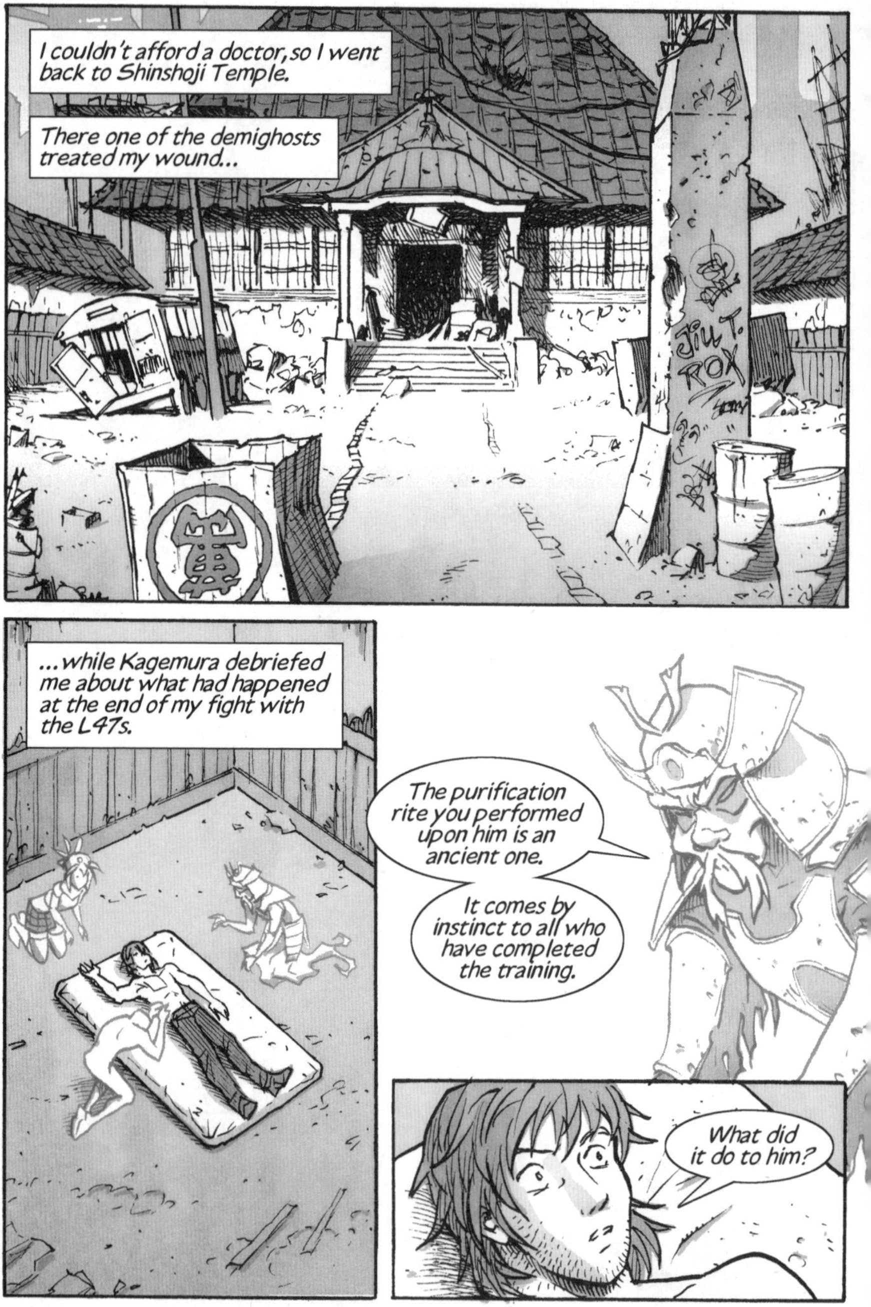
I couldn't afford a doctor, so I went back to Shinshoji Temple.
There one of the demighosts treated my wound...
JIU T. ROX
...while Kagemura debriefed me about what had happened at the end of my fight with the L47s.
The purification rite you performed upon him is an ancient one.
It comes by instinct to all who have completed the training.
What did it do to him?

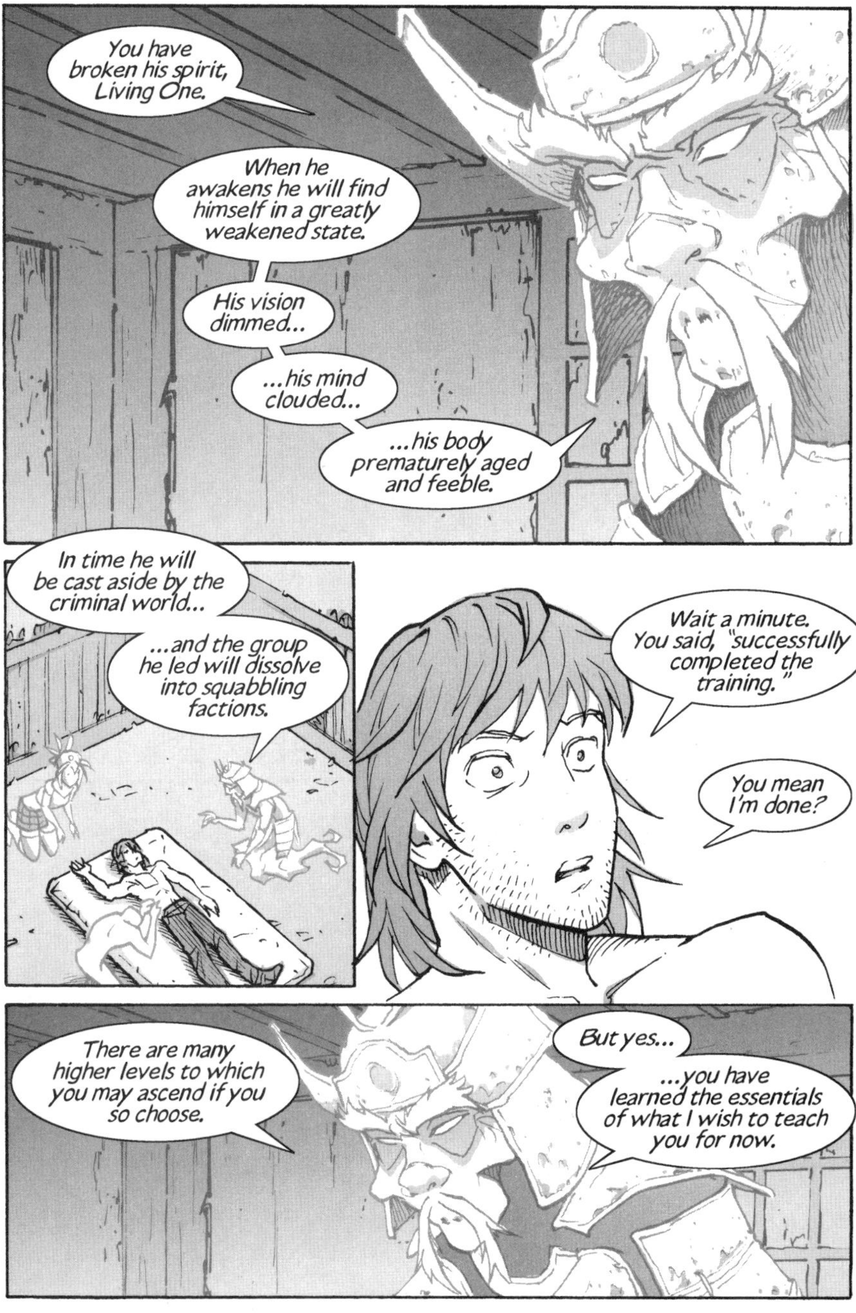
You have broken his spirit, Living One.
When he awakens he will find himself in a greatly weakened state.
His vision dimmed...
...his mind clouded...
...his body prematurely aged and feeble.
In time he will be cast aside by the criminal world...
...and the group he led will dissolve into squabbling factions.
Wait a minute. You said, "successfully completed the training."
You mean I'm done?
There are many higher levels to which you may ascend if you so choose.
But yes...
...you have learned the essentials of what I wish to teach you for now.

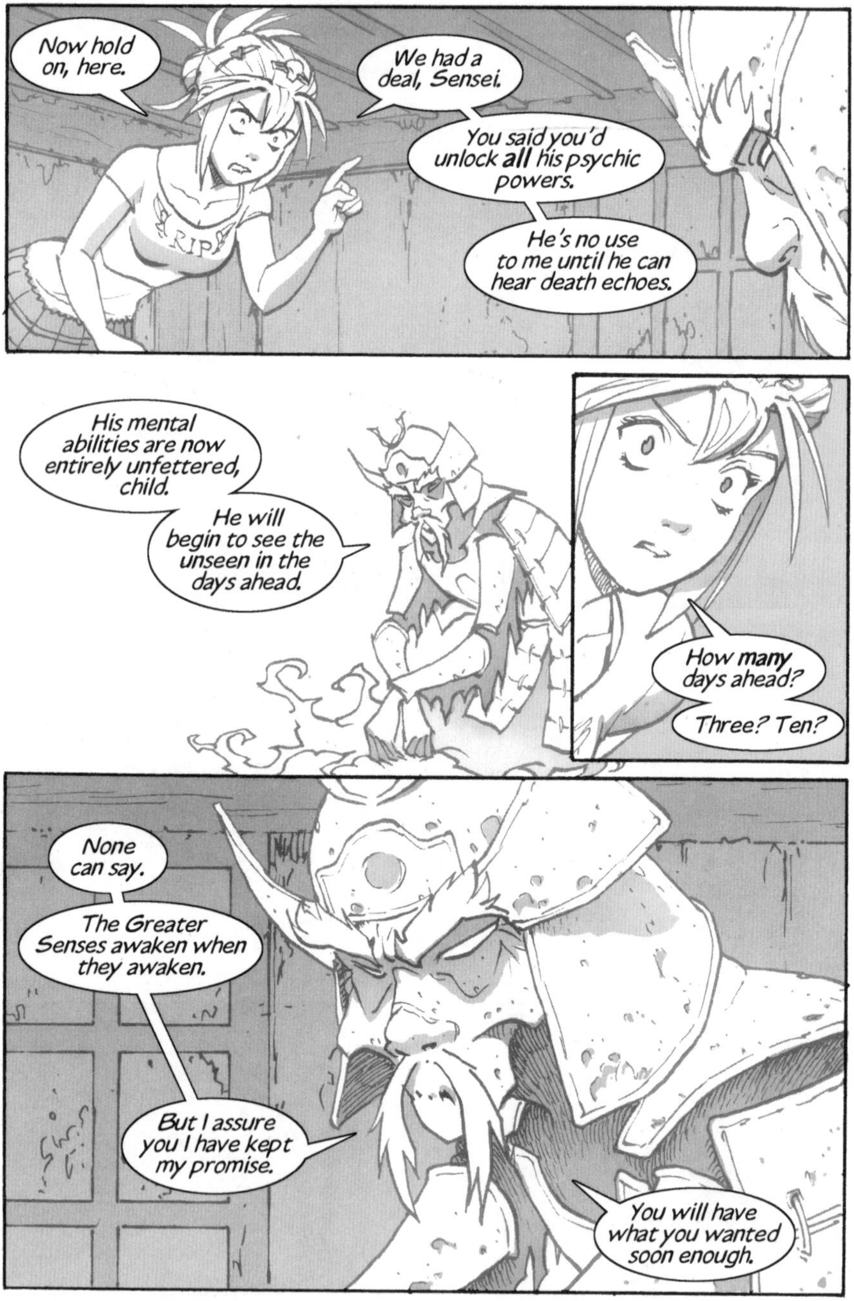
Now hold on, here.
We had a deal, Sensei.
You said you'd unlock **all** his psychic powers.
He's no use to me until he can hear death echoes.
His mental abilities are now entirely unfettered, child.
He will begin to see the unseen in the days ahead.
How **many** days ahead?
Three? Ten?
None can say.
The Greater Senses awaken when they awaken.
But I assure you I have kept my promise.
You will have what you wanted soon enough.

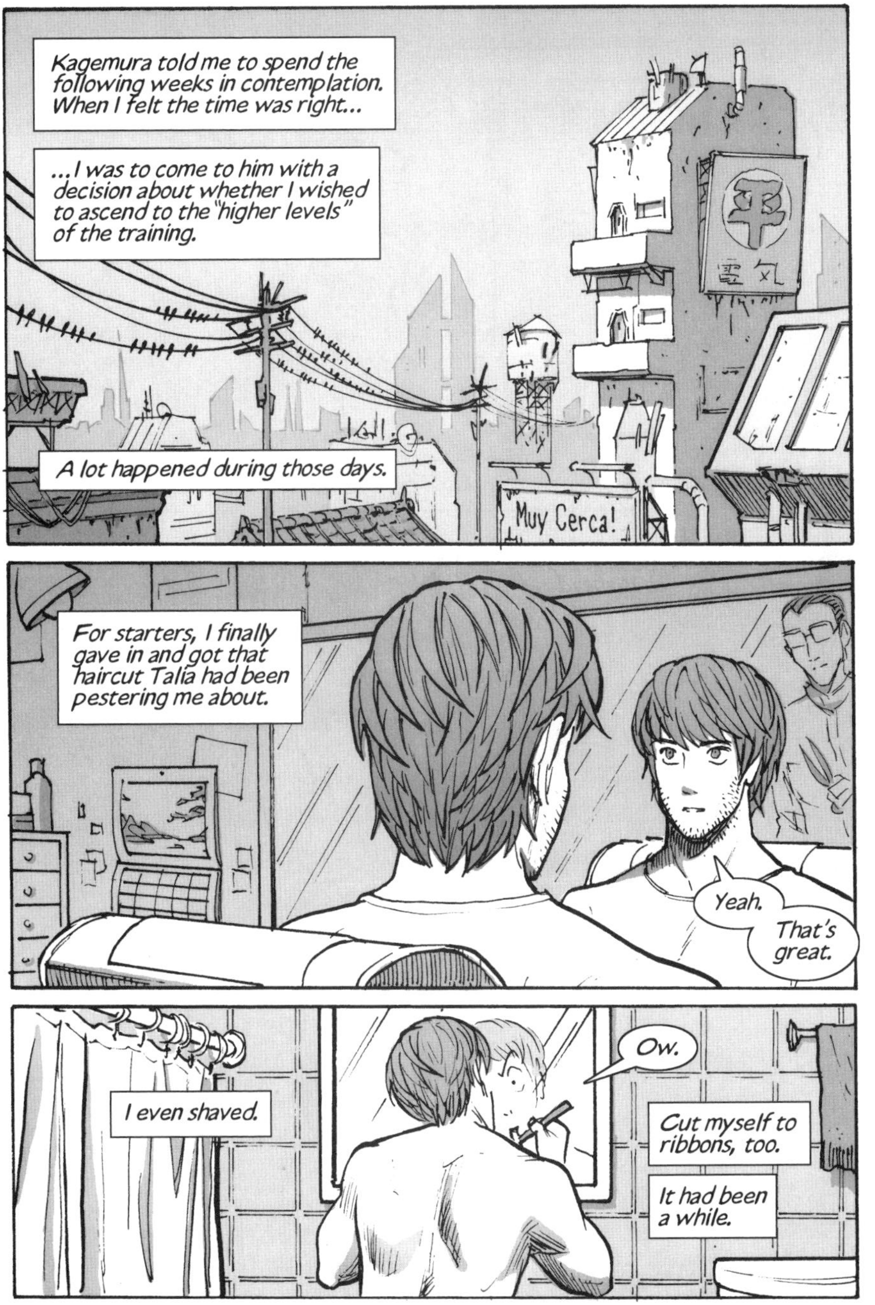
Kagemura told me to spend the following weeks in contemplation. When I felt the time was right...
...I was to come to him with a decision about whether I wished to ascend to the "higher levels" of the training.
A lot happened during those days.
Muy Cerca!
For starters, I finally gave in and got that haircut Talia had been pestering me about.
Yeah.
That's great.
I even shaved.
Ow.
Cut myself to ribbons, too.
It had been a while.

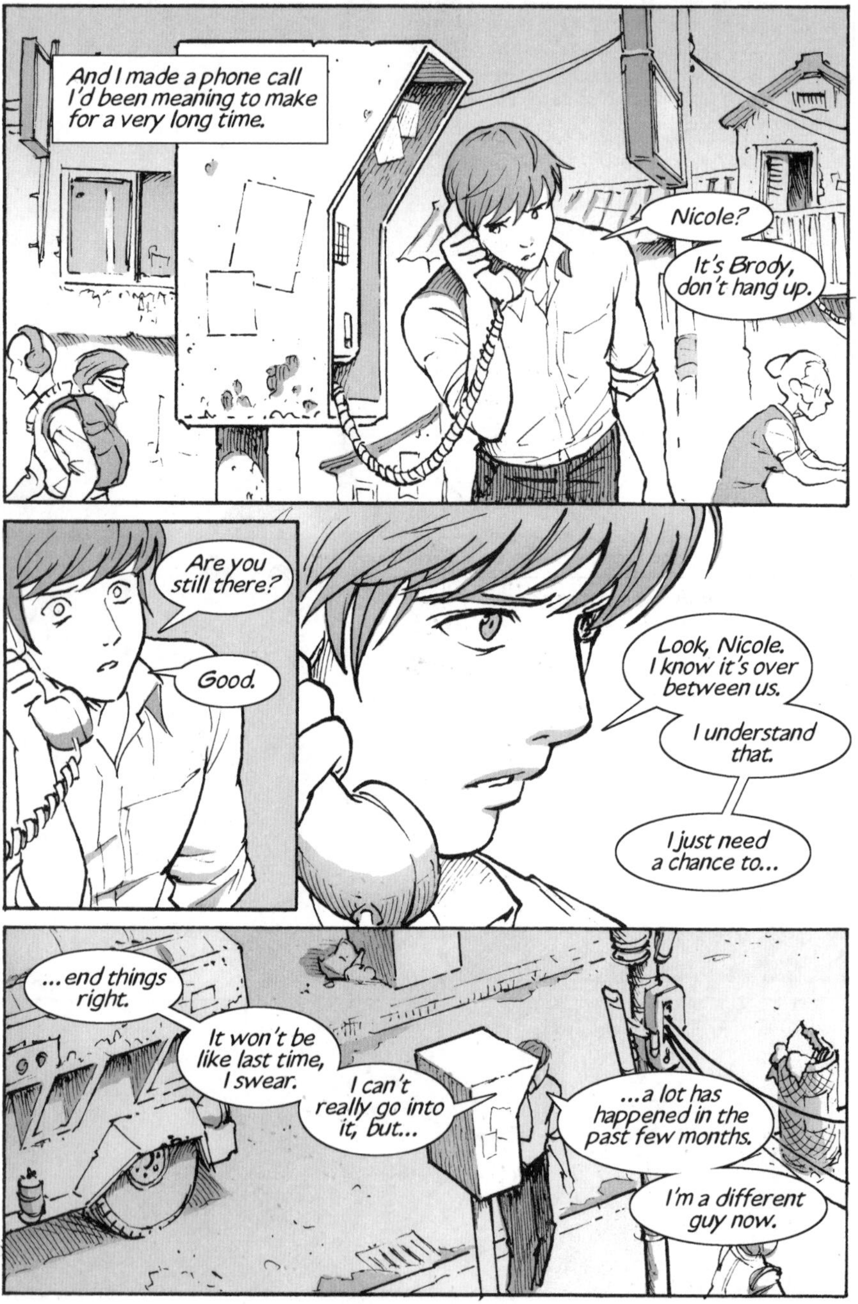
And I made a phone call I'd been meaning to make for a very long time.
Nicole?
It's Brody, don't hang up.
Are you still there?
Good.
Look, Nicole. I know it's over between us.
I understand that.
I just need a chance to...
...end things right.
It won't be like last time, I swear.
I can't really go into it, but...
...a lot has happened in the past few months.
I'm a different guy now.

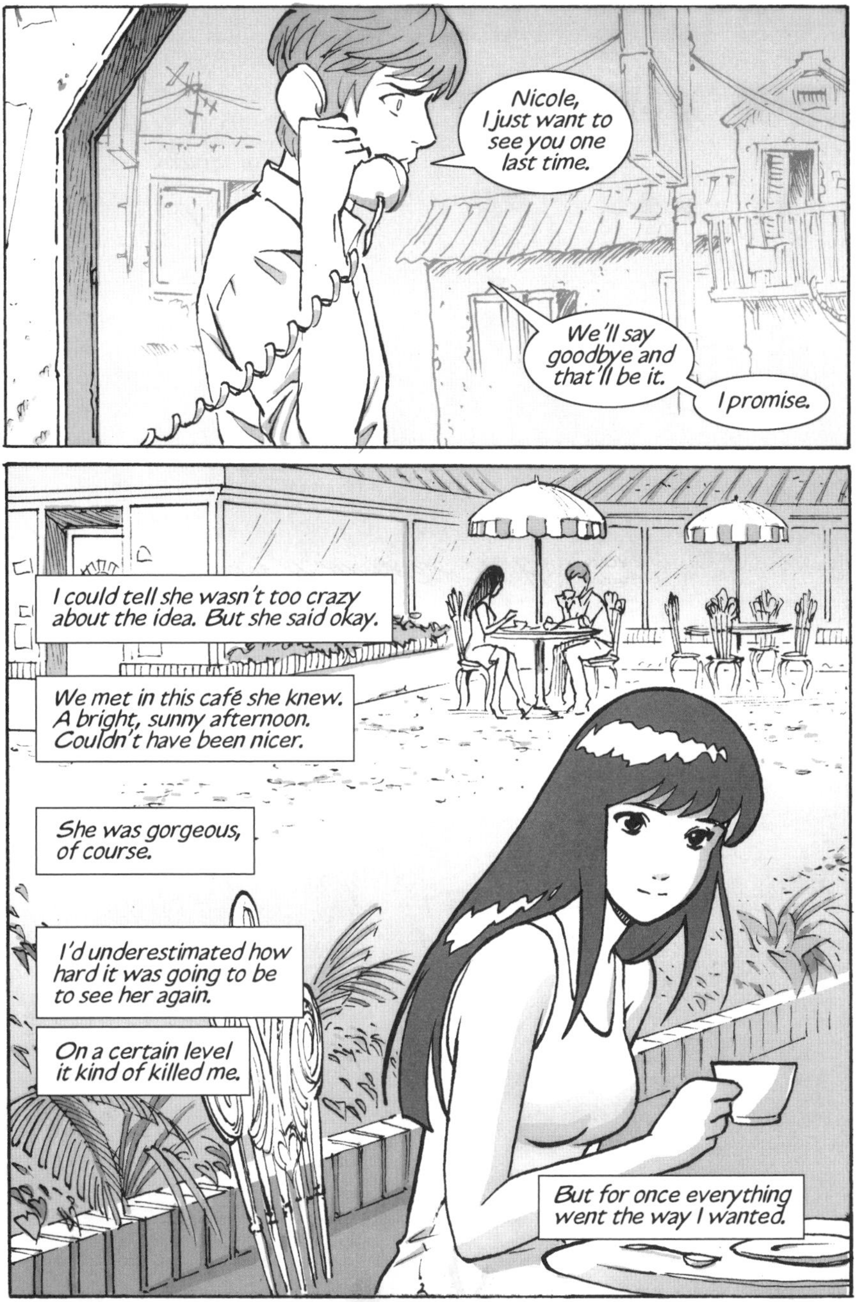
Nicole, I just want to see you one last time.
We'll say goodbye and that'll be it.
I promise.
I could tell she wasn't too crazy about the idea. But she said okay.
We met in this café she knew. A bright, sunny afternoon. Couldn't have been nicer.
She was gorgeous, of course.
I'd underestimated how hard it was going to be to see her again.
On a certain level it kind of killed me.
But for once everything went the way I wanted.

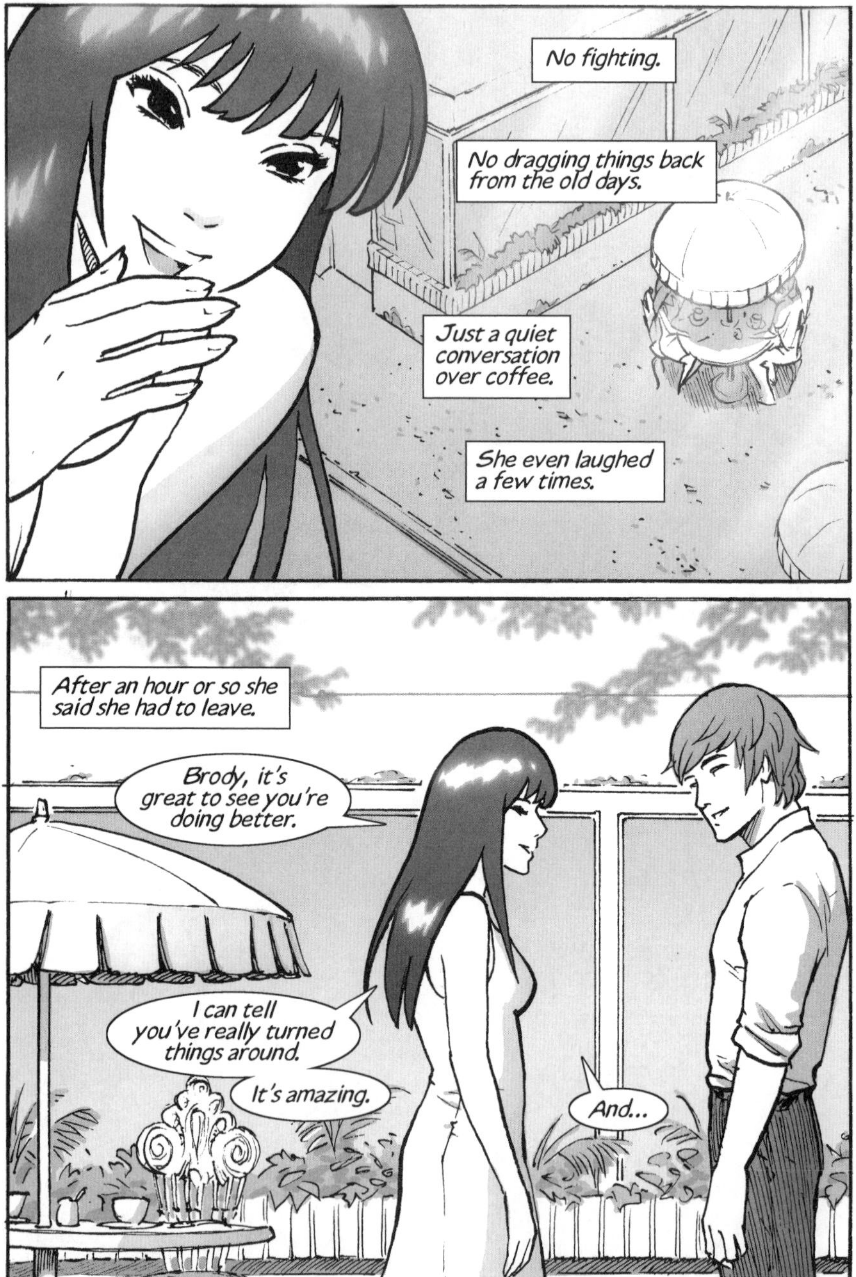
No fighting.
No dragging things back from the old days.
Just a quiet conversation over coffee.
She even laughed a few times.
After an hour or so she said she had to leave.
Brody, it's great to see you're doing better.
I can tell you've really turned things around.
It's amazing.
And...

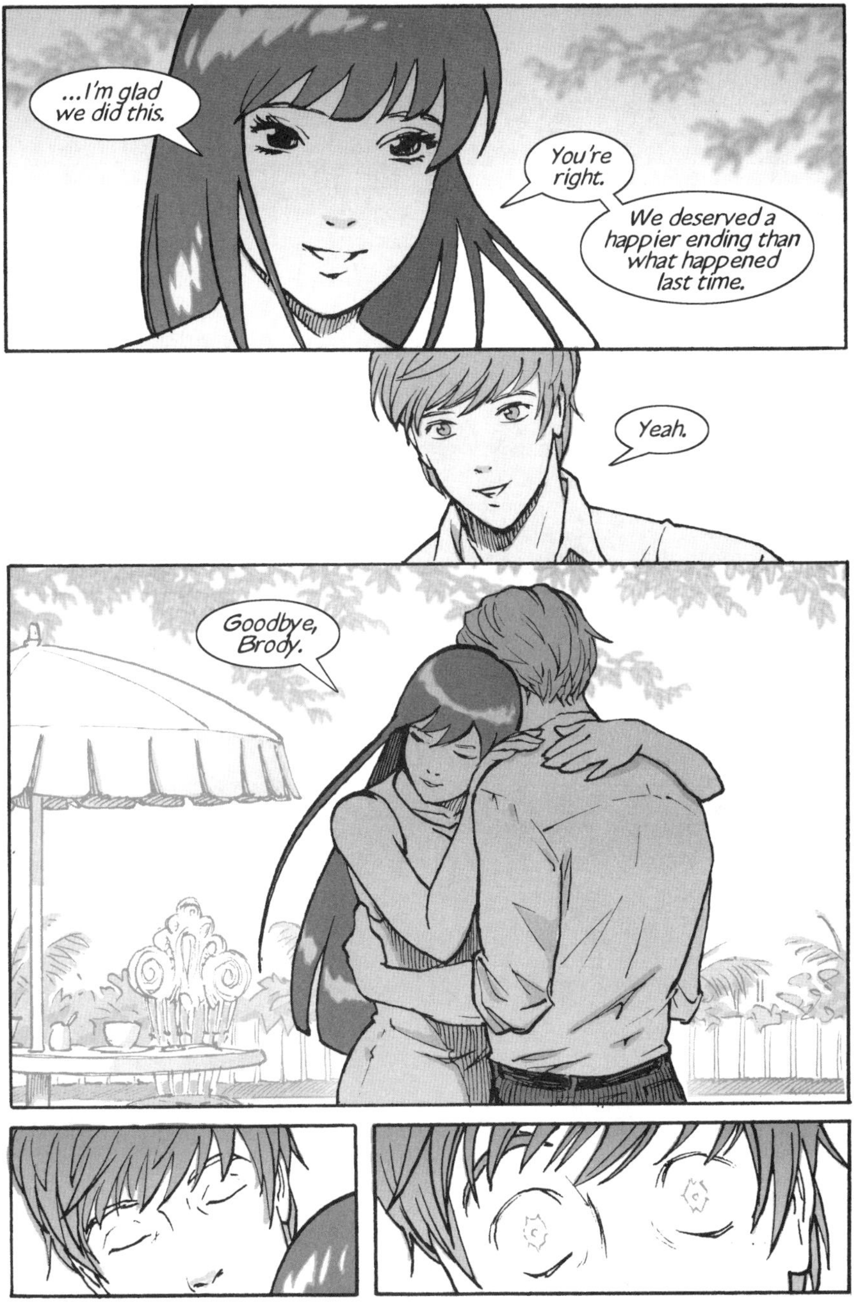
...I'm glad we did this.
You're right.
We deserved a happier ending than what happened last time.
Yeah.
Goodbye, Brody.

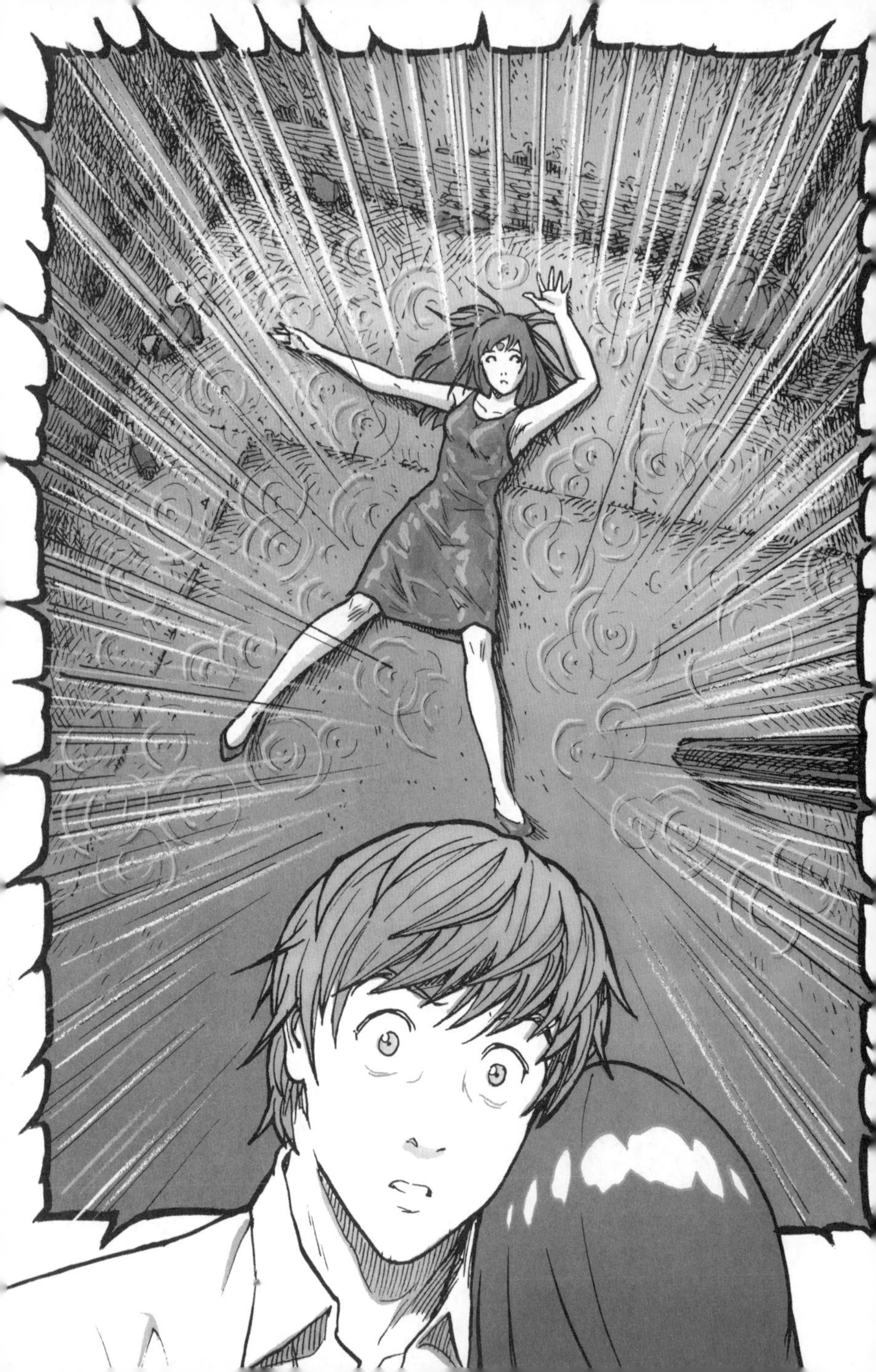

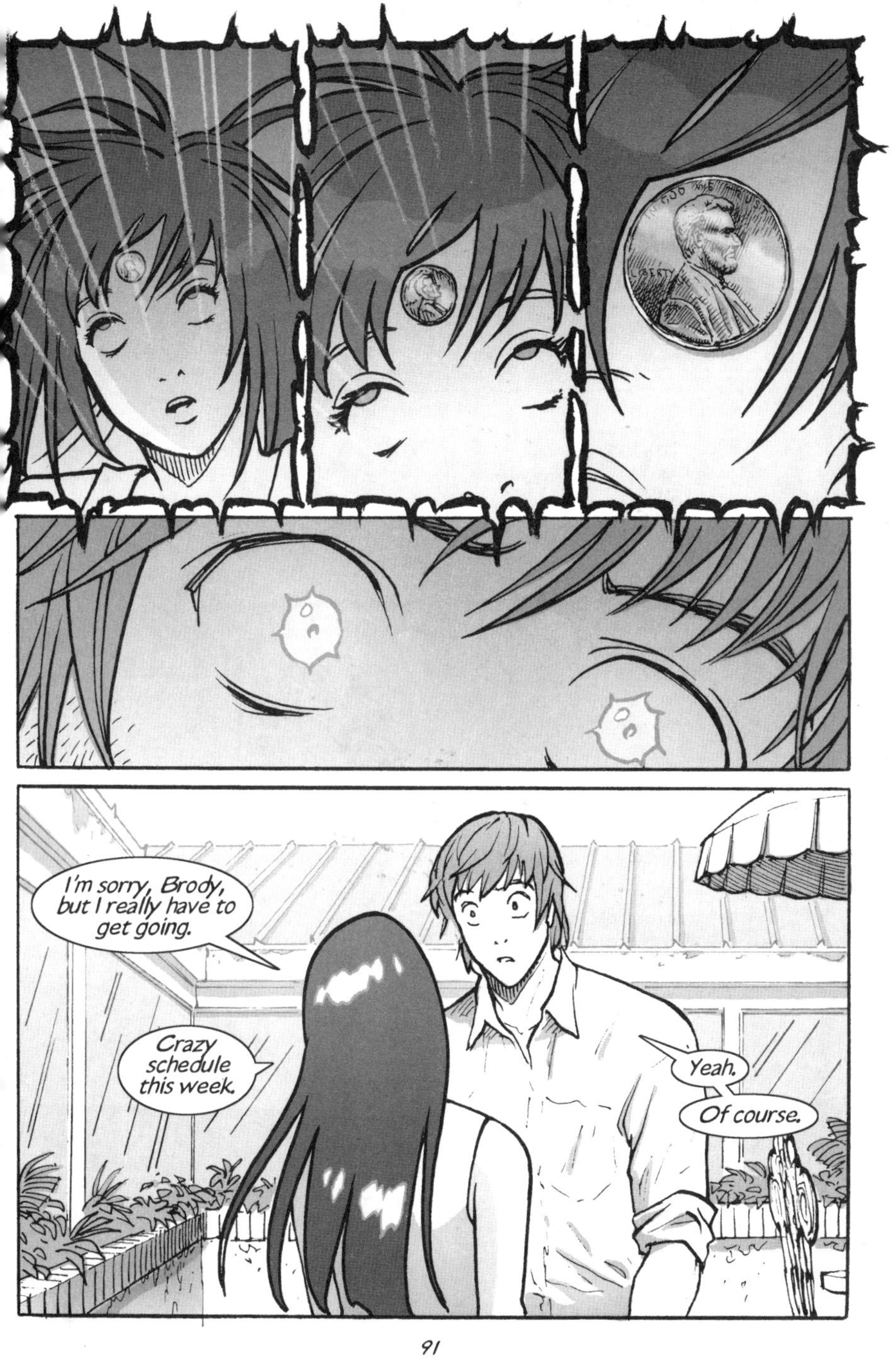
I'm sorry, Brody, but I really have to get going.
Crazy schedule this week.
Yeah.
Of course.

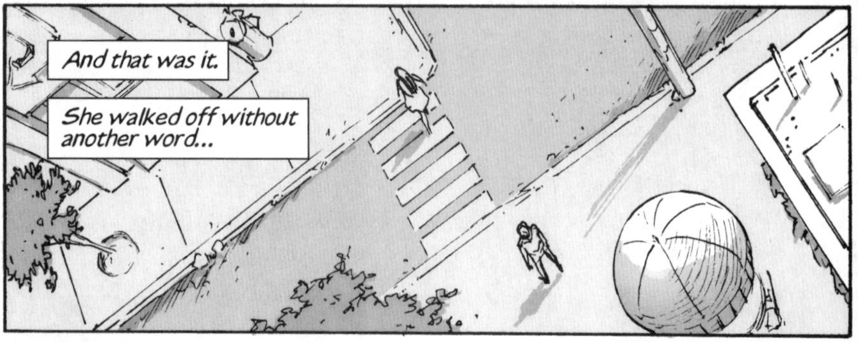
And that was it.
She walked off without another word...

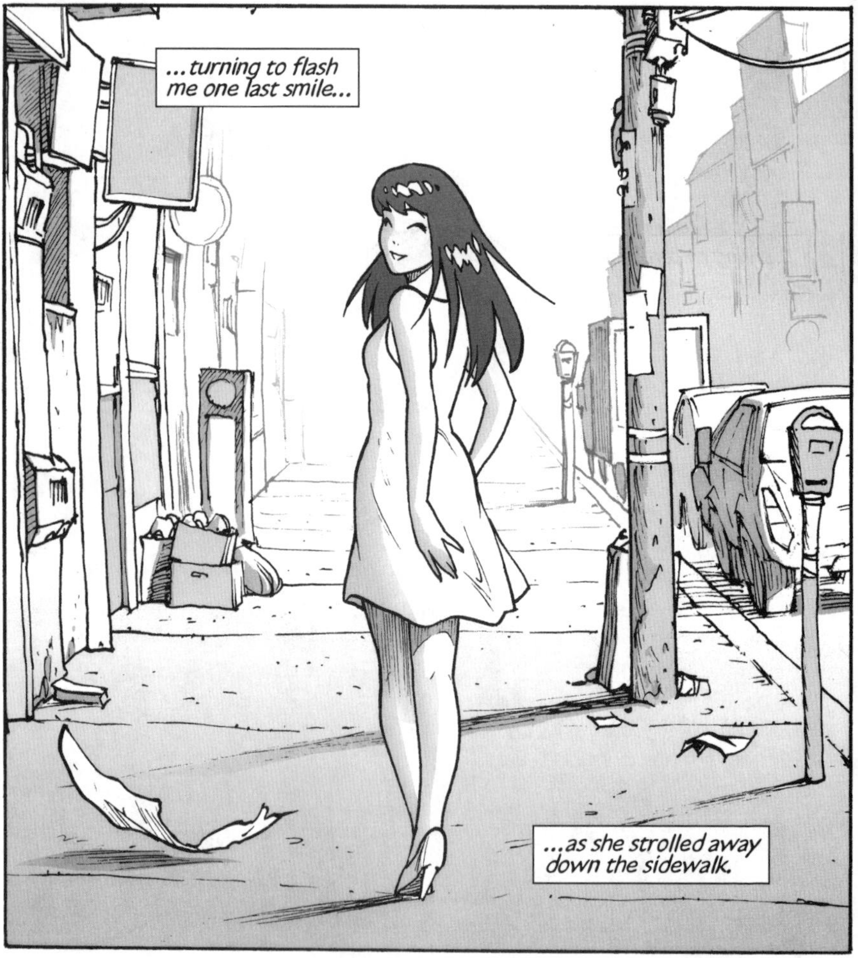
...turning to flash me one last smile...
...as she strolled away down the sidewalk.

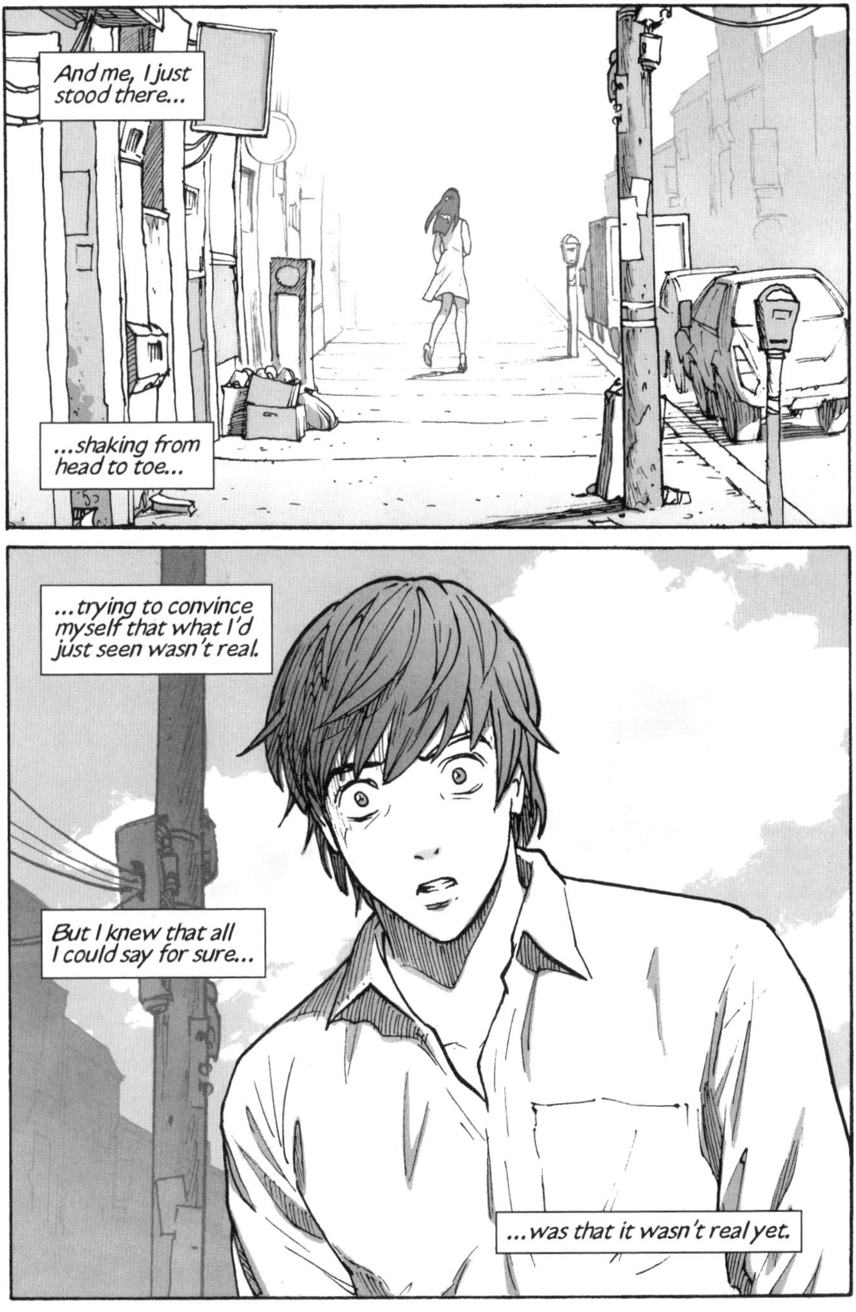
And me, I just stood there...
...shaking from head to toe...
...trying to convince myself that what I'd just seen wasn't real.
But I knew that all I could say for sure...
...was that it wasn't real yet.

TO BE CONTINUED IN BRODY'S GHOST BOOK THREE...

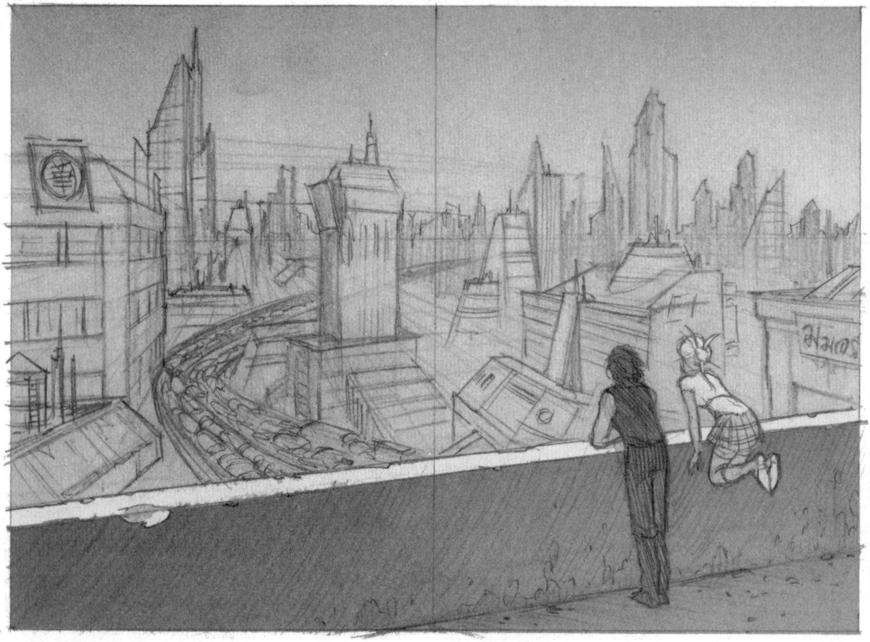

I knew Brody's Ghost *Book 2 would need at least one double-page spread to remind readers of the futuristic urban locale of the series. At first I thought I'd put Brody and Talia on the roof of the parking garage and give us their view of the city, but somehow the composition lacked drama (above). Thus was born the final spread, in which the cityscape overtakes the entire surface of both pages, dwarfing our main characters and giving readers more details to examine.*

Often my rough pages leave an awful lot to the imagination. This establishing shot of the L47s' headquarters (right) is so sketchy I was in effect asking my editor to take a leap of faith: "This will look a lot better in the final book, honestly!"

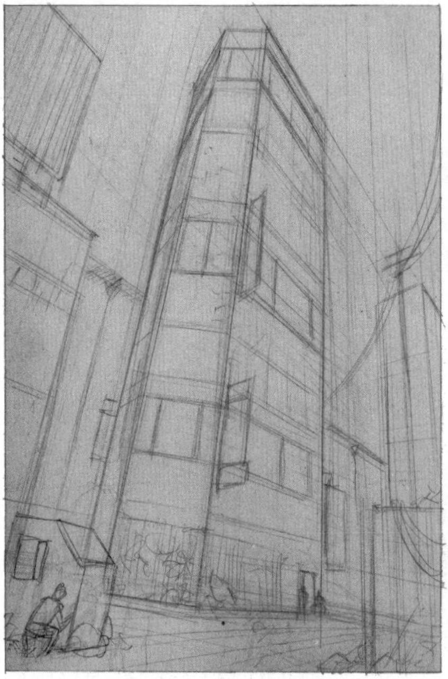

In Brody's second flashback I originally had an image of him with his arms outstretched (below). Feeling it lacked intensity, I instead had him preparing to smash a lamp on the floor: a more frightening way, I thought, of conveying his rage.

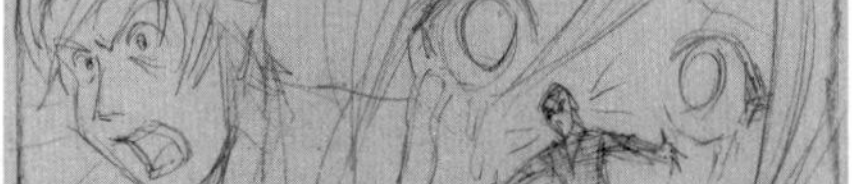

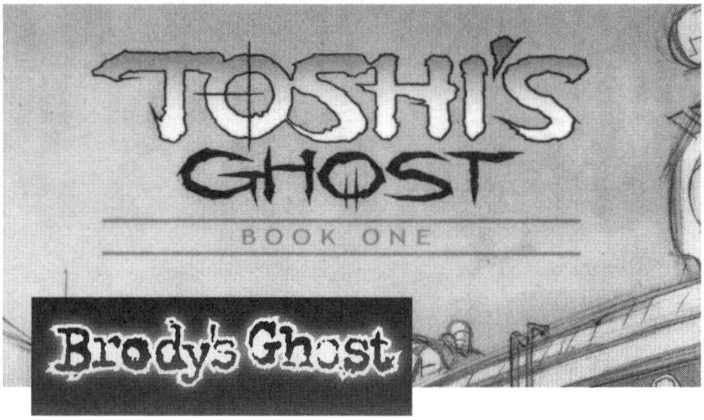
TOSHI'S GHOST
BOOK ONE
Brody's Ghost

Not many people know that Brody's Ghost *was originally set in futuristic Tokyo with an all-Japanese cast of characters. Hence the first title I came up with:* Toshi's Ghost. *I even got as far as designing a logo before changing the name (left). Now only Kagemura remains as evidence of the story's Japanese origins.*

The logo design also went through many changes. Here you see what I came up with (inset, left) before handing the logo-design reins to Scott Cook at Dark Horse, who created the logo you now see on the cover.

Early on I toyed with the idea of giving Talia a little "ghost assistant" who would float alongside her at all times: never speaking, but sometimes perpetrating acts of mischief against Brody. She was to have been named Chanpopo-chan (right), and would have been the only character in the series drawn in the Japanese chibi style.

I soon realized there was simply no room in the story for this character, and so she never even made it as far as the first draft. I still kind of like the design, though!

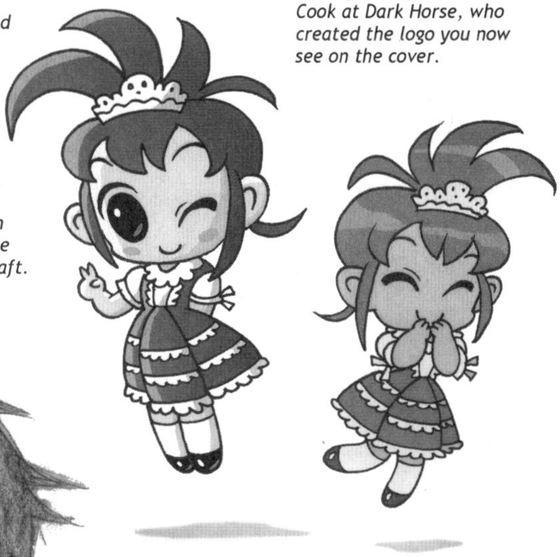

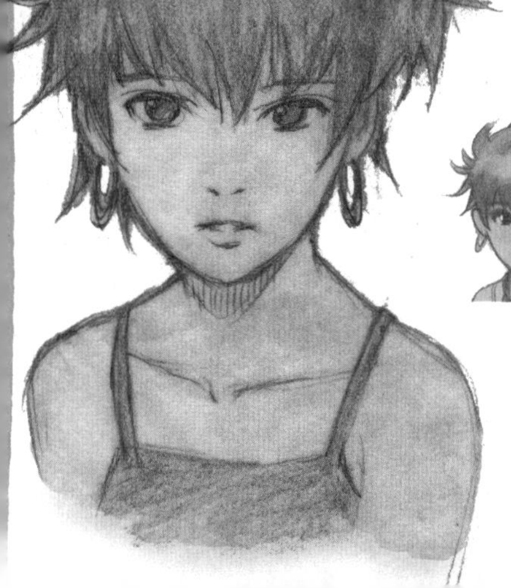

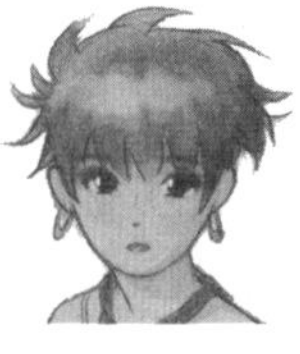

For quite a while I envisioned Brody's ex-girlfriend Nicole as having short hair. I wanted her to convey the air of a certain type of fashion model, making bold choices in her clothing and jewelry.

As time went on I realized that this hairdo--meant to be stylish--might instead end up looking just as messy as Brody's, and we couldn't have that! Somehow the longer hairstyle I opted for also resulted in ditching the whole "fashion model" vibe and letting her beauty come across as something more natural and effortless.

HOW TO DRAW TALIA

The trick to drawing Talia--or any character, really--is getting all the lines in the right spot. For the beginning artist it's best to start with a few penciled guidelines.

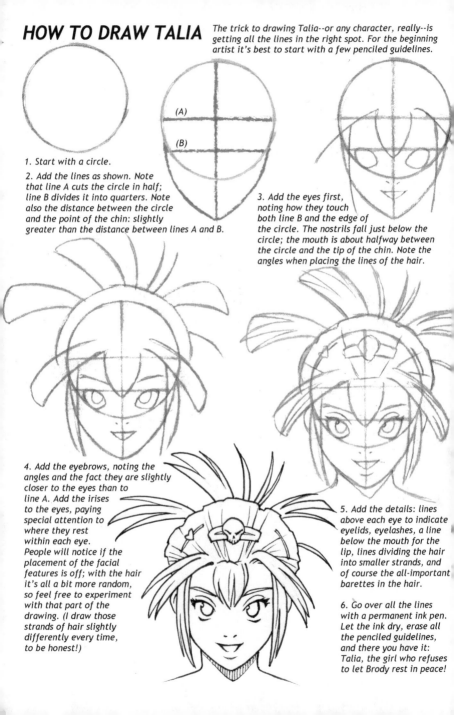

(A)

(B)

1. Start with a circle.

2. Add the lines as shown. Note that line A cuts the circle in half; line B divides it into quarters. Note also the distance between the circle and the point of the chin: slightly greater than the distance between lines A and B.

3. Add the eyes first, noting how they touch both line B and the edge of the circle. The nostrils fall just below the circle; the mouth is about halfway between the circle and the tip of the chin. Note the angles when placing the lines of the hair.

4. Add the eyebrows, noting the angles and the fact they are slightly closer to the eyes than to line A. Add the irises to the eyes, paying special attention to where they rest within each eye. People will notice if the placement of the facial features is off; with the hair it's all a bit more random, so feel free to experiment with that part of the drawing. (I draw those strands of hair slightly differently every time, to be honest!)

5. Add the details: lines above each eye to indicate eyelids, eyelashes, a line below the mouth for the lip, lines dividing the hair into smaller strands, and of course the all-important barettes in the hair.

6. Go over all the lines with a permanent ink pen. Let the ink dry, erase all the penciled guidelines, and there you have it: Talia, the girl who refuses to let Brody rest in peace!